EXPLORE
COPENHAGEN

D0027533

CONTENTS

SHOPPERS

Resist temptation in the department stores on Strøget (route 2) and Kongens Nytorv (route 3), the boutiques off Strøget, in Nørrebro (route 7), and the independent shops in Vesterbro (route 1).

RECOMMENDED ROUTES FOR...

DESIGN COPENHAGEN

Lap up serious modern design at Illums Bolighus on Strøget (route 2). The Radisson Blu Royal is a design icon (route 1) and Designmuseum Danmark has wonderful displays (route 4).

FOOD AND WINE

Copenhagen has 15 Michelin-starred restaurants. Værnedamsvej (route 1) is Copenhagen's gourmet food street, while Magasin du Nord (route 3) offers an excellent food hall.

CHILDREN

Treat the kids to a trip to Tivoli (route 9), day or night, and watch their fascination grow at the zoo (route 8) or Experimentarium City (route 11). Be dazzled by the crown jewels at Rosenborg (route 5).

HANS CHRISTIAN ANDERSEN

Wander through his stamping ground around Kongens Nytorv and Nyhavn (route 3). Visit the Bakkehuset (route 1), The Little Mermaid (route 4) and the Church of Our Lady where his funeral was held (route 2).

ART ENTHUSIASTS

Explore the National Gallery (route 6), the Ny Carlsberg Glyptotek (route 9), the Thorvaldsens Museum (route 10) and Rosenborg (route 5). Outside the city visit the Arken, Ørdrupgaard and Louisiana galleries (route 14).

RENAISSANCE ARCHITECTURE

Visit the Round Tower and Trinity Church (route 2), Rosenborg Castle (route 5), Kastellet and Nyboder (route 4), the Stock Exchange (route 10) and Christianshavn (route 11).

ROYALISTS

Follow in the steps of kings at Slotsholmen (route 10), Rosenborg (route 5), Church of Our Lady (route 2), Amalienborg (route 4) and Roskilde (route 12). Don't miss the Royal Copenhagen store (route 2).

INTRODUCTION

An introduction to Copenhagen's geography, customs and culture, plus illuminating background information on cuisine, history and what to do when you're there.

Copenhagen has over 300km (186 miles) of cycle paths

EXPLORE COPENHAGEN

Copenhagen is a pretty seaside city with a thriving nightlife, the sophisticated gastronomic and cultural offerings of a far larger city and a visible history going back 900 years.

Copenhagen (København), the capital of Denmark, is located on the eastern side of Sjælland (Zealand), the largest of Denmark's 407 (named) islands, with only the Øresund (Sound) separating it from Sweden. It was founded by Bishop Absalon in 1167, and these days, including its greater metropolitan area, is home to about 1.2 million of the country's estimated 5.63 million people. The smaller municipality of Copenhagen – made up of 15 districts that extend beyond the geographical scope of this book – accounts for approximately 747,000 inhabitants.

STRATEGIC LINK TO EUROPE

Connected by the south of Jutland to Germany, Denmark is the only Scandinavian country physically joined to the European mainland and, as such, is the bridge between Scandinavia and the rest of the continent. It is also literally the bridge to Sweden with the Øresund road and rail bridge linking it with the city of Malmö.

Consequently, Denmark shares many of the characteristics of its Nordic neighbours: liberal welfare benefits coupled with a high standard of living, and a style of government that aims at consensus and the avoidance of petty bureaucracy. Yet Denmark is also more 'European' and accessible than the rest of Scandinavia, and its appeal is universal.

THE CITY

With its strategic location at the mouth of the Baltic Sea, Copenhagen has always been an important hub and, as such, a tempting prize for pirates and traders. As a small fishing village in the 12th century, it attracted the protection of Bishop Absalon and the dastardly attentions of Wendish pirates. One century later, German traders of the Hanseatic League were pounding on its doors. By the 15th century, the Sound was even more of a cash cow with its herring salted and exported all over Europe and the king charging a toll on every ship that passed on its way to the Baltic.

Over the centuries, Copenhagen grew but always, even today, remained reasonably compact, its residents moving out gradually from the central conurbation. In the 12th century, Slot-

sholmen was the centre; by the Middle Ages, the town had expanded across the water to the banks of what is now the Old Town.

The medieval citizens put up walls surrounded by a moat, which enclosed the city to the north, east and west. With the exception of Østerport (East Gate), which stood on Gothersgade until the 17th century, near to what is now Kongens Nytorv, the gates in the walls were on or near the sites still called Nørreport (North Gate) and Vesterport (West Gate). The fortress of Slotsholmen and the watery boundary of the Sound stood to the south. The five reservoirs to the north are all that remain of the medieval moat.

In the 16th century, under the aegis of Christian IV, the city's fortifications were extended east. The fortress Kastellet (see page 52) was built, and the East Gate and rampart were located next to it, thus bringing Rosenborg (1606–34) within the walls and practically doubling the amount of space inside the city walls in what was known as 'New Copenhagen'. To the south, Christianshavn (see page 84) was built up and a series of new islands created with naval yards and protective bastions. Nyboder, near Østerport, was built to house the naval workers. At the same time, Christian IV created some of the most lasting buildings of the entire city, including Rosenborg Castle, Kastellet, Børsen and the workers' district of Nyboder. Boasting

an elegant Renaissance style, they are still standing today.

One century later, the city expanded again, as Frederiksstad (see page 47) was built in 'New Copenhagen' on the land acquired by Christian IV. It was (and is) the most aristocratic area in town, and was constructed on the site of a former royal country palace that had burnt down. On the banks of the Sound, Kongens Nytorv was developed and Nyhavn was excavated and the merchants built their houses along its wharfs, to be close to the precious goods in their warehouses.

Fire was always a threat in a town made of wood, and the 18th century saw two shocking blazes that destroyed

The Danes

Copenhagen's inhabitants are as appealing as their city; liberal, generally law-abiding, socially responsible (just look at their generous social security system, paid for with huge taxes that few complain about), gregarious, and – at the same time – charming and sarcastic. They are skilled at enjoying life, especially when it comes to *hygge*, a word that loosely translates as a combination of warmth, well-being and intimacy, usually involving the combination of family, friends, food and copious amounts of alcohol. They are also informal in dealing with people and put a lot of focus on their personal freedom.

Looking down on pedestrianised Strøget

almost the whole of the medieval centre. With the odd exception (including, fortunately, most of Christian IV's marvellous buildings), what the visitor sees today is 18th-century neoclassical architecture.

By the 19th century, Copenhagen was too compact: it was packed with people and had no sanitation to speak of; certainly not enough to deal with the effluence that the heaving city spat out daily. In 1853, cholera broke out, killing several thousand people, including the well-known Golden-Age artist, Christoffer Eckersberg.

In 1856, the old ramparts were pulled down to improve conditions and the populace spread into the countryside, which soon became the districts of Nørrebro, Vesterbro, Østerbro and Frederiksberg (although this is still technically a separate municipality from Copenhagen).

Thanks to the architect and town planner Ferdinand Meldahl (1827–1908), these districts were conserved as the parks that ring the inner city today, stretching from Kastellet, via Østre Anlæg behind the National Gallery of Art, the Botanical Gardens and Ørsteds Parken. Tivoli, also once part of the ramparts, was the work of entrepreneur George Carsten in 1843 (see page 77).

COPENHAGEN TODAY

The 20th and 21st centuries have seen further changes to the city. The old quarter was pedestrianised from the 1960s; the docks are being rejuvenated; and the authorities have taken a particular interest in updating the city's landscape with startling modern structures such as the Black Diamond library extension (1999), the Harbour Baths (2003–11), the Opera House (2005), the Royal Danish Playhouse (2008), the DR Koncerthuset (2009), and the Blue Planet aquarium (2013). A whole new 'downtown' area, Ørestad, has been created from scratch on Amager island, and other areas of the suburbs are undergoing huge regeneration. Another ambitious project is the expansion of the Metro. The circular Cityringen line, made up of 15.5km (9.6 miles) of track with 17 new stations, is due to open in 2019. Many of the city's most weird and wonderful designs were dreamed up by innovative architecture firm BIG Copenhagen (www.big.dk) – see their website for future plans.

Copenhagen districts

As in most large cities, different areas can be categorised by the sort of people (and incomes) that tend to populate them. Indre By, the inner city covering an area of 9 sq km (2,200 acres), has a population of c.51,000. The quietest part of the Old Town is the financial district behind Kongens Nytorv and Holmens Kanal, where fewer than 500 people live – there are generally more visitors gently snoring away every night than there are locals.

The Botanical Gardens   *Café culture*

More than half the apartments in this area are occupied by affluent young singles. They're also popular with those in the 50-plus age bracket, who want to be close to the city centre's cultural opportunities.

DON'T LEAVE COPENHAGEN WITHOUT...

Riding Tivoli's 100-year-old wooden rollercoaster. Tivoli pleasure gardens contain one of the world's oldest rollercoasters. Even fuel rationing in World War II couldn't stop Rutschebanen from rolling along the tracks: all two tonnes of it were hauled to the top of the lift hill by hand. See page 77.

Sipping a cool beer on the 'sunny side' of Nyhavn. Colourful 17th-century houses and old wooden sailing ships provide the perfect backdrop for alfresco wining and dining. Nyhavn is an attractive street, often called Copenhagen's longest bar. See page 45.

Testing the next generation of city bikes. Found at docking stations around the city, Copenhagen's Bycyklen have built-in GPS and electric motors for when the pedalling gets tough. See page 134.

Winding your way to the top of the Rundetårn. This 17th-century astronomical observatory is a one-of-a-kind structure, set amongst the cobbled maze of Copenhagen's beautiful old Latin Quarter. See page 39.

Exploring the Louisiana Museum of Modern Art. Denmark's most-visited museum is a work of art in itself, its beautifully designed buildings surrounded by a sculpture garden overlooking the sparkling sea. It has a fabulous international collection, including works by Picasso, Giacometti, Miró and Henry Moore, as well as homegrown favourites like Asger Jorn. See page 101.

Eating smørrebrød. The Danish open-faced rye-bread sandwich is a work of art, whether it's a modern miniaturised 'smushi' version (see page 42) or the country's favourite 'Stjerneskud' (Shooting Star). See page 15.

Seeing the filming locations of Borgen and The Killing on Slotsholmen. Christiansborg Slot, home of the Danish parliament as well as many museums, will seem very familiar to fans of DR's gripping television dramas. Nordic Noir Tours (www.nordicnoirtours.com) run walking tours visiting locations of The Killing, The Bridge and Borgen from Vesterport Station on Saturdays at 2pm and 4pm. See page 78.

Climbing the tower of Vor Frelsers Kirke. A wooden staircase made up of 400 steps twists its way around the outside of the church's baroque spire, getting narrower and narrower as it does so. Not for anyone with vertigo, but the sure-footed and clear-headed will be rewarded with spectacular city views. See page 86.

Taking a dip in the harbour. Perhaps you were hypnotised by the glittering water after taking one of the worthwhile boat tours up and down Copenhagen's waterways (see page 46). If so, grab your swimsuit and head for the open-air Islands Brygge harbour baths, a fabulous place to hang out in summer. See page 22.

Students and young families tend to live in Nørrebro or Vesterbro, which are also Copenhagen's most multicultural areas. Nørrebro has a population of almost 78,000 and is the most densely populated district. In recent years, it has seen more social problems than other parts of the city; nonetheless, it has the reputation for being a cool place to hang out. Once-seedy Vesterbro is now respectably edgy: over the last few years, a young, creative crowd has moved in and transformed the old meat-packing district, Kødbyen, into a hub of stylish new bars, clubs, restaurants and galleries.

Christianshavn is Copenhagen's little Amsterdam, surrounded by water; according to one commentator, it was 'built for rich people, taken over by poor people and is now radical chic'. The arrival of affluent newcomers attracted by its regeneration has caused some resentment among the locals.

Østerbro and Frederiksberg are more upmarket; there are several embassies in Østerbro, including those of the US, Canada, Great Britain and Russia.

AN ECO-FRIENDLY CITY

These days, Copenhagen is still a compact city and, for the visitor, eminently walkable or bicycle-friendly. The Danes cycle in their thousands: men in suits, students, mums with babies in cart extensions, even people cycling with pets. It makes for a city with clear air, few traffic jams, healthier people, an impression of safety and a satisfying sense of doing something for the planet.

Copenhagen has a deserved reputation as the most bicycle-friendly city in the world. 41 percent of all journeys are made by bike, and there are 400km (248 miles) of cycle paths with more planned. The city council devotes around DKK 250 million of its annual budget to cycling. Special carriages for bikes on trains enable cyclists to combine biking with travelling on public transport more easily.

The emphasis on being eco-friendly becomes clear before you even set foot in Copenhagen. Look out of the aeroplane as you approach the airport, and you can't fail to see the massive Middelgrunden wind farm – the world's biggest when it opened in 2000 – in the Sound. Wind turbines such as these supply around 41 percent of all Denmark's electricity. The Sound itself is clean enough to swim in, and many of its beaches have been awarded Blue Flag status. The authorities are very active: they have decreed that 90 percent of all food served in the city's public institutions will be organic by 2015, and that all citizens will be able to walk to a park in under 15 minutes. Copenhagen also has a very ambitious programme of recycling, with plans to limit non-recyclable materials to two percent of household waste.

The Black Diamond, Slotsholmen

TOP TIPS FOR EXPLORING COPENHAGEN

Current events. For up-to-date Copenhagen listings, check out the Visit Copenhagen tourist office website (www.visit copenhagen.com), or pick up a copy of the free weekly English-language newspaper, *The Copenhagen Post* (www.cphpost.dk), available from tourist offices and some hostels.

Free attractions. Entry is free at all times to the permanent collections at the National Museum and The National Gallery of Denmark (including the Music History Museum and the Royal Cast Collection), and to the intriguing Post & Tele Museum. There is free admission on Wednesdays to Thorvaldsens Museum, and on Sundays to the Ny Carlsberg Glyptotek. It costs nothing to look at the statue of the Little Mermaid, people-watch in Christiania, or swim and sunbathe at Amager Beach. Copenhagen has some lovely parks and gardens where you can wander at will, including those around Rosenborg Castle, the nearby Botanical Gardens and romantic Frederiksberg Gardens.

Copenhagen Card. If you have kids in tow and plan to see a lot of sights, the Copenhagen Card (www.copenhagencard.com) is very good value; it allows free transport and entry to sights for up to two children under the age of ten for every adult card. There are also children's cards available for 10–15 year-olds.

Changing of the Guard. Don't miss this colourful demonstration of Danish pomp and ceremony. Amalienborg Palace is guarded by the Royal Life Guards *(Den Kongelige Livgarde)*. At around 11.30am each day, the guards march from their barracks at Gothersgade 100 (by Rosenborg Castle) to Amalienborg, where the Changing of the Guard ceremony takes place.

Plan ahead for Roskilde Festival. Tickets to Northern Europe's biggest music festival, held in late June/early July, go on sale from the 1st December.

Bring comfy shoes. The best way to see Copenhagen is by walking, but all those cobbles can be hard on the feet – make sure you bring suitable footwear for a blister-free visit.

Look out for bicycles. It might sound obvious, but pedestrians should take care when crossing cycle lanes. Copenhageners cycle fast, and if you aren't paying attention, you could easily cause an accident.

Tipping. Tipping is not the norm. However, no-one will complain if you reward excellent service!

Free Wi-fi. Many cafés, bars and hotels across the city have free Wi-fi, as does the Copenhagen Visitor Centre at Vesterbrogade 4A, across from Tivoli Gardens.

Go Green! Copenhagen aims to become the world's first carbon neutral city by 2025. The Discover Green Copenhagen map, available at tourist offices, shows you where to find eco-friendly restaurants, cafés, hotels and shops. See www. visitcopenhagen.com for information.

Chefs at work

FOOD AND DRINK

Denmark is a gastronome's delight. Try beautifully prepared smørrebrød, or treat yourself to a New Nordic tasting menu – Copenhagen now has more Michelin-starred restaurants than any other city in Scandinavia.

Traditional Danish food, as you would expect from a seafaring nation in a cold, murky climate, was based around sturdy, filling dishes of carbohydrates, meat and fish. In this generally agricultural and seafaring nation, people produced food from what they grew themselves or was available locally, using ingredients such as apples, beer, bread, cereals, carrots, dairy products, pork, onions, plums, potatoes and seafood. Dishes were seasonal in spring and summer but in the long, cold, dark winters, they depended on ingredients that had been preserved from the harvest seasons, using techniques such as pickling and salting. In the days of no refrigeration, it was these foods – ones that could be stored almost indefinitely – that came to dominate the country's traditional dishes.

These days, Danish food, especially in restaurants, has lightened up. With more contact with foreign cultures and food through holidays, immigration and greater food marketing and availability, the Danes, like the inhabitants of much of the rest of Europe, have become increasingly familiar with foreign dishes and ingredients. Leading the way is

a generation of young chefs who are proponents of the New Nordic Cuisine manifesto, with its emphasis on showcasing the bounty of northern Europe by using local, organic, seasonal produce. Armed with these fresh ingredients, some have reinvented traditional Danish dishes for a modern palate, while others have combined them with more exotic tastes from abroad to create a new 'fusion' cuisine (especially French, Italian and Thai).

DAILY MEALS

A traditional Danish breakfast, or *Morgenmad*, involves bread and butter, cheese, possibly cold meats and coffee. Porridge and beer-and-bread porridge (*Øllebrød*) are also very occasionally eaten. Of course, many people also eat cereal. Coffee is generally drunk rather than tea. In a hotel, the sheer scope of choice can be overwhelming, especially if faced with plates and plates of small Danish pastries *(wienerbrød)*.

Lunch, or *Frokost*, can vary, but most people have an open sandwich or *smørrebrød*. This is traditionally a piece of dark rye bread with a topping.

A delicate starter at Studio

Diners at GRO rooftop farm

These can be quite complicated: *Dyrlæ-gens natmad* ('Veterinarian's midnight snack'), for example, consists of liver paté *(leverpostej)*, topped with corned beef *(salt kød)* and a slice of meat aspic *(sky)*, plus raw onion rings and cress.

Other traditional sandwich toppings include smoked eel, scrambled egg and radishes; chopped liver paté with bacon and sauteed mushrooms; thin slices of roast pork *(ribbensteg)* with red sweet-and-sour cabbage; *gravadlax* (slices of smoked or cured salmon on white bread with shrimp, lemon and fresh dill); and, perhaps most complex of all, *Stjerne-skud* ('Shooting Star'), which consists of two pieces of fish (one steamed, one fried and battered) on a piece of buttered white bread, piled high with shrimp, mayonnaise, red caviar and a slice of lemon.

A traditional alternative to *smørrebrød* is to eat from a *Dansk Kold Bord*, or Danish Cold Table. Some restaurants offer these, though it is very typical at home on festive occasions. The cold table is like a buffet, with a cold first course, usually some sort of marinated herring *(mar-inerede sild)*, which might be pickled or served up in a red or white vinegar dressing. Sour cream sauces are also popular. On extra-festive occasions, the herring might be prepared with other ingredients, such as potato, onions and capers topped with a dill sour cream/mayonnaise sauce. Herring is usually served with ice-cold snaps, which, according to the Danes, helps it to swim down to the stomach. Danish snaps *(akvavit)* is

usually flavoured with caraway seed, at least 75 percent proof, and tends to be cheaper than imported spirits.

The second course will be cold meats and salads, followed by a warm dish, usually on a piece of rye bread, followed by cheese and biscuits.

Supper is called *Middag* because it used to be eaten in the middle of the day. It is eaten at home and most Danes make an effort to gather the family around a hot meal every evening. Meat is usually served, often with traditional gravy and potato dishes, although international foods, such as pasta, pizza and American-influenced foods are also popular.

EATING AT HOME

Food plays an important part both in the Danish psyche, as it brings people together, and in the concept of 'hygge', a term hard to translate but meaning something along the lines of 'cosiness, warmth and comfort with good food, drink and company', although it can mean different things to different people. Eating together is an important social event, whether it is a daily family affair or a dinner with non-family guests.

As in most places, there are traditional times of year that the family comes together if it can. In Denmark, a Christmas lunch *(Julefrokost)* and an Easter lunch *(Påskefrokost)* are traditional. The Christmas table or *Julebordet* is organized like a *Kold Bord*, and, in addition to everyday *smørrebrød* toppings, there

A feast for the eyes and the tastebuds

will be special Christmas dishes such as *æbleflæsk* (pork slices served with an apple, onion and bacon compote), *flæsk-esteg* (roast pork with crackling) and *Julesylte*, a pork paté served with pickled beetroot and mustard.

Other traditional foods include goose (though many people now prefer duck), eaten on 24 December with boiled potatoes, pickled red cabbage, tiny caramelised potatoes and gravy and, for pudding, *Ris à l'amande*, a rice pudding served with whipped cream, chopped almonds and cherry sauce. Traditionally, everyone eats until someone finds the whole almond hidden in the pudding. This dish was served first as, in the past, it was used to fill everyone up, so that a small amount of meat would go around. The meal is usually washed down with beer or *snaps*.

EATING IN RESTAURANTS

In Copenhagen, there are over 2,000 restaurants and cafés, which will usually provide a good meal. There are also those that will provide something extraordinary: 15 Copenhagen restaurants were awarded 17 Michelin stars in 2014. René Redzepi's New Nordic restaurant Noma was also bestowed once more with the title of "World's Best Restaurant" by the prestigious *Restaurant Magazine*.

Copenhagen's cafés are usually open from the morning until late at night, and make especially cosy corners for curling up with coffee and cake. Most serve alcohol and will provide food throughout the day and into the evening, and some turn into clubs with music and dancing at night. If you prefer bartenders to baristas, cocktail joints have become very popular in recent years – go for a 1920s classic or experiment with contemporary Copenhagen creations such as the Spotted Pig (at Salon 39, Vodroffsvej 39) or the champagne-based Lavender Dew (at Ruby, Nybrogade 10).

Restaurants are usually a bit more formal and the kitchen will close a couple of hours before the last people are expected to leave. If you want to eat late, always ring to find out when the kitchen closes. Restaurants that serve both lunch and supper often stop serving in the late afternoon, so don't be surprised if lunch is not available after about 2pm. For smart restaurants, it is always advisable to book ahead.

WHERE TO BUY FOOD

If you want to buy food yourself, Copenhagen has some excellent food stores. Dubbed a 'gourmet street', Vesterbro's **Værnedamsvej** is a wonderful place to find delicatessens, a high-quality butcher, greengrocer, and wine, cheese and chocolate shops. If you don't get that far, all the department stores are generally worth a visit for their upmarket grocers.

For organic bread, pâtisserie, wine, chocolate and oil check out one of the many **Emmerys** stores (central outlets

Traditional smørrebrød

include Østerbrogade 51; Vestergade 13; Store Strandstraede 21; www.emmerys. dk). The new wave of organic delicatessens includes the renowned **Meyers Deli** (Kongens Nytorv 13; Gammel Kongevej 107; Godthåbsvej 10; www. meyersdeli.dk). Those with a sweet tooth should head for one of the **Lagkagehuset** pâtisseries (Frederiksberggade 21; Vesterbrogade 4a; Ny Østergade 12; Frederiksborggade 6) to sample Danish cakes and pastries. A growing number of microbreweries offer thirsty travellers pilsner-type beers, from Tivoli's own **Færgekroen Bryghus** (Vesterbrogade 3; www.faergekroen.com) to the prizewinning Nørrebro Bryghus (Ryesgade 3; www.noerrebrobryghus.dk).

The city's biggest indoor market Torvehallerne, near Nørreport metro station, has 60 stalls selling fresh produce, as well as sushi, tapas and porridge stands.

The *pølsevogn* (sausage wagon) is a fast-food institution in Copenhagen. Hotdogs, including the infamous long red sausages *røde pølser*, are served with bread, mustard, ketchup and remoulade, and washed down with chocolate milk.

Eco-labelling

The Danish mark of inspection for organic products is a red 'Ø' symbol. This indicates that the product has been inspected by the Danish authorities and must meet stringent quality and production regulations. A product can only be marketed as organic if 95 percent of its ingredients are certified by the 'Ø' symbol. The same conditions apply to products bearing the 'Euro-leaf' logo, the EU's official organic label used throughout Europe. The EU flower symbol and the Nordic Council of Ministers' stylised swan symbol are common eco-labels, used on non-food products that do not contain any toxic ingredients and that have been manufactured with the least possible impact to the environment.

Traditional Dishes

Æbleflæsk Pork slices with an apple, onion and bacon compote.

Æggekage 'Egg cake': a substantial omelette-like dish, sometimes made with flour so it rises slightly.

Biksemad Beef hash served with a fried egg and ketchup.

Blodpølse Black pudding, made from pig's blood.

Brændende Kærlighed Called 'Burning Love', this is mashed potato with fried onion and pieces of bacon.

Finker Sweetmeat similar to haggis.

Flæskesteg Roast pork with crackling (*svær*).

Frikadeller Meatballs, Denmark's 'national' dish.

Millionbøf Tiny pieces of beef in gravy, poured over mashed potato. The name means 'million steak'.

Øllebrød Porridge made of rye bread, sugar and beer.

Stegte sild i eddike Fried herring in vinegar.

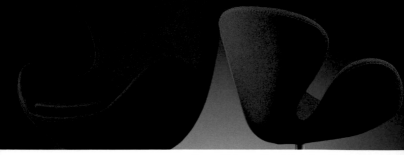

The world-famous Egg chair designed by Arne Jacobsen

SHOPPING

Copenhagen is an appealing, if not especially cheap, place to shop, especially for Danish designer goods, particularly furniture, household items and clothing. Whether you buy or not, it's a great place for window-shopping.

THE SHOPPING MAP

With plenty of cafés and street entertainment, and over a kilometre of pedestrianised streets, Strøget makes for a stress-free shopping experience. The quality of the goods in its mainstream shops improves as you head up the street from Rådhuspladsen, reaching a rather smart conclusion up by Kongens Nytorv, with designer boutiques and furriers such as Prada, Gucci and Louis Vuitton, and Danish designers SAND and Birger Christensen.

Vimmelskaftet, Amagertorv and Østergade are home to some of Denmark's most famous names. Here you'll find Lego's flagship emporium; the 120-year-old department store Illums; its sister store, Illums Bolighus, which will fulfil all your designer desires for household gadgets and wonderful Danish furniture and lighting; Royal Copenhagen, with its world-famous china (and the opportunity to paint your own plate or cup, see page 37); Georg Jensen, the father of simply designed silver jewellery (at a price); and Hay House, an important stop for minimalist furniture and colourful rugs.

Magasin du Nord, an elegant department store located on Kongens Nytorv, will take care of your sartorial needs. Up the road, Danish audio wizards Bang & Olufsen have their main store.

Do not be afraid to wander off Strøget into the streets adjoining it, as it is here that you will find lots of independently owned, quirky little shops. Tucked off the main thoroughfare are gems such as Stilleben at Niels Hemmingsensgade 3, which sells unusual homeware and hand-made ceramics; or Norse Store at Pilestræde 41, a must for fashion-conscious chaps.

Farvergade, Kompagnistræde and Laederstræde run parallel to Strøget in one uninterrupted pedestrian street, lined with shops dealing in oriental rugs, antique furniture, silverware, china and curios. The prices aren't exactly low, but on a good day it's possible to find a fair deal. These streets are more popular than Strøget among Copenhageners and the cafés are always full of people. On Laederstræde, check out Grønlykke (No. 3) for funky and kitsch home furnishings. Hidden away in a basement next door at No. 5 is Wettergren & Wettergren, whose owners update vintage

Inside the Copenhagen-based Munthe plus Simonsen store

clothing and accessories. For girlie presents, such as pastel porcelain and flowery cushions, try Liebe at No. 23 Kompagnistræde,

The Latin Quarter, close to the university, is home to several book shops *(boghandel)* and second-hand clothing and record shops. There are flower stalls round the back of Magasin du Nord; for a more exotic floral experience, have a look in the window of designer florist Tage Andersen at Ny Adelgade 12.

Kronprinsensgade, north of Strøget, contains many of Denmark's designer clothes shops, like the exclusive Bruuns Bazaar at No. 9.

Away from the centre

Elsewhere, there are plenty of opportunities to seek out independent little shops. Out in Nørrebro, for example, around Sankt Hans Torv, you will find antique and bric-a-brac shops on Ravensborggade, vintage clothing on Blågardsgade and young, eclectic clothes shops run by aspiring designers in streets such as Elmegade – try design collective Fünf at No. 2, Stokkel at No. 3 for shoes and accessories, or Radical Zoo at No. 19 for edgier Danish fashion.

Nansensgade near the reservoirs is an up-and-coming area, with a smattering of interesting shops and cafés.

Better still is trendy Vesterbro: Istedgade boasts various boutiques run by young artists and designers, some still experimenting with their styles. Long-standing favourites include Donn Ya Doll at No. 55, with a mouthwatering choice of 30 clothes designers; and Kyoto at No. 95, with a cool selection of understated Scandinavian fashion. In the same district, Designer Zoo (Vesterbrogade 137) showcases the creations of seven Danish designers, who work on the premises in glass, ceramics, wool and gold, plus changing works from 20 to 40 invited artists.

If you are after authentic antiques, Bredgade near the Amalienborg is full of shops and auction houses. However, the largest destination for antiques is Green Square in Amager (Strandlodsvej 11B).

DANISH HOUSEHOLD DESIGN

Danish furniture ranks among the world's best. Here you'll see items credited to the designer rather than to the factory. Furniture is a national pride and most good pieces will have a black circular 'Danish Furniture-Makers' sticker attached. Lamps are also lovingly designed, as are household textiles and hand-woven rugs.

If you want your shops under one roof, the best places are Illums Bolighus (Amagertorv 10; www.illums bolighus.dk), Casa (Store Regnegade 2; www.casagroup.com) or, north of Osterbrø, the designer furniture store, Paustian (Kalkbrænderiløbskaj 2; www.paustian.dk).

The Royal Theatre stalls

ENTERTAINMENT

There is lots to do in the evenings in Copenhagen, above and beyond eating out. This section features general information about the main concert venues and nightlife hotspots; for individual bar and club listings, see page 122.

TIVOLI

An evening visit to **Tivoli** (see page 77) is a must, even if it is just for a wander to take in the lights, fireworks and the atmosphere. If you wish to be a little more focussed, the open-air stage has free evening concerts on Fridays. There is also an impressive concert hall, with an aquarium containing sharks and tropical fish in the foyer.

CONCERT HALLS

The **Tivoli Concert Hall** (tel: 33 15 10 12; www.tivoli.dk) is one of the largest classical venues for ballet, opera and classical music in Copenhagen; it also puts on rock concerts and is a major venue during the jazz festival in July. You will need to book in advance.

The Danish Symphony Orchestra were treated to a fabulous new home in 2009: the **DR Koncerthuset** (Emil Holms Kanal 20; tel: 35 20 62 62; www.dr.dk/koncerthuset) on Amager, designed by Frenchman Jean Nouvel, is a jaw-dropping piece of architecture and the most expensive concert hall ever built. Its spaces are used for pop, rock and jazz as well as classical concerts.

THEATRE, OPERA AND DANCE

There are several places on offer – some more dependent on an understanding of Danish than others. **The Opera House** (Operaen; Ekvipagemestervej 10, Holmen; tel: 33 69 69 69; www.operaen.dk; see page 88) is a wonderful evening out offering both traditional and modern opera and ballet in a startling building. The auditorium is very comfortable with excellent visibility and acoustics. Ticket prices vary from 125dkk in the gods to 895dkk in the stalls.

Its sister venue the **Royal Theatre** (Det Kongelige Teater; tel: 33 69 69 69; www.kglteater.dk) puts on some concerts and ballets, but its functions have mostly been superseded by the Opera House and the more modern **Royal Danish Playhouse** (Skuespilhuset; Kvæsthusbroen; tel: 33 69 69 33; www.kglteater.dk), on the waterfront near Nyhavn. It has two big stages – the main stage with 650 seats and Portscenen with 200 seats – together with a studio stage, restaurant, café and a large public square in front of the build-

ing with harbour views. For some performances the north wall can be opened up on to the quayside. Almost half the building is constructed in the water, partly on new fill and partly on detached piles.

The **New Theatre** (Det Ny Teater; Gammel Kongevej 29; tel: 33 25 60 05; www.detnyteater.dk) just off Vesterbrogade does a roaring trade in big musicals such as *West Side Story*, *My Fair Lady*, *Phantom of the Opera* and *Beauty and the Beast*.

JAZZ CLUBS AND DINNER-DANCES

Copenhagen has a bit of a reputation for jazz, with a renowned 10-day international festival held from the first Friday of July onwards. The **Copenhagen Jazz House** (the city's premier jazz spot), Jazz House Montmartre and **Mojo's** (a smaller, more intimate venue) should tide you over until festival time.

If you fancy an all-in-one bit of entertainment, try out **Wallmans Saloner** (Cirkusbygningen, Jernbanegade 8; tel: 33 16 37 00; www.wallmans.dk; Thu–Sat from 5.30pm; show 7pm–11.15pm, dancing to 1am; prices from 529dkk), where your evening takes in a four-course meal and stage entertainment (glamorous dancers, singers and acrobats), followed by a night of dancing.

BARS, CLUBS AND DISCOS

Copenhagen has plenty of cool drinking places, from rustic bistros to chic modern bars to cosy cellar pubs. Danes take pride in their lager-style beers, and there are several excellent brew-pubs, such as **Nørrebro Bryghus**, where you can sample beer made on the premises. Copenhageners love a cocktail – you'll find plenty of shaking and stirring going on around town.

There are no shortage of places to dance the night away, including many late-opening cafés and bars. **Vega**, in Vesterbro, is one of the oldest and biggest nightclubs. Vesterbro is also where you'll find the former butchers' district Kødbyen, which has seen an incredible reinvention over the past few years and is now one of the city's hottest areas for wining, dining and partying. New places are still opening there, such as the massive KB III nightclub. The city's edgier areas, such as Nørrebro, have a large share of up-and-coming bars, and grungier clubs such as **Rust**, which offers live bands and international DJs.

Of course, the best parties are the ones that you stumble upon accidentally – ask the locals.

LISTINGS

For listings of what is going on in Copenhagen, including cinema listings (most films are shown in their original version with subtitles), check out The Copenhagen Post (www.cphpost.dk), the English-language weekly newspaper. Visit Copenhagen (www.visitcopenhagen.com) also has a diary of events.

A solar-powered GoBoat

ACTIVITIES

Copenhagen has sporting activities to suit every taste, from open-air swimming in the summer to ice-skating in the winter. The top spectator sport is football (soccer), while popular participation sports often involve water.

SWIMMING

There are about a dozen indoor swimming pools in Copenhagen, some with sauna/massage and gym facilities, and several open-air pools which are usually open from June to August. So successful has the clean-up of the Inner Harbour been that there is now a fantastically popular outdoor bathing area at Islands Brygge (open June–Aug 7am–7pm), with five pools (two just for kids), three diving towers and a green lawn packed full of picnickers in front. There are plans to create saunas and thermal baths so the area can open year-round.

Another wonderful facility is Amager Strandpark (tel: 33 66 33 19; www.amager-strand.dk), a vast artificial beach and lagoon just 5km (3 miles) south of the city centre, where Copenhageners flock to swim, run, row, skate, and play beach volleyball. There are Metro stations at three places along the beach: Øresund, Amager Strand and Femøren.

Last but not least, the sandy Svanemølle Beach and its 130-metre (423ft) -long pier were constructed in 2010 to the delight of the residents of Østerbro. The beach has lifeguards during July and August.

WATERSPORTS

Kayaking and boat hire

You can hire kayaks from Kayak Republic (http://kayakrepublic.dk), based near Holmens Kirke, to explore the city's canals (guided tours are also available). Groups of six or more can have a go at kayak polo – contact Kayakole (tel: 40 50 40 06; www.kajakole.com) at Amager Strandpark. Also at Amager Strandpark, you can rent kayaks and canoes from Kajakhotellet (http://kajakhotellet.dk).

Another eco-friendly option is to hire one of the solar-powered "picnic boats" from GoBoat (www.goboat.dk), situated next to the Islands Brygge swimming pools. These cute little crafts chug along the city's canals at a leisurely three knots.

Wakeboarding and kite-surfing

You can learn to wakeboard in a safe environment at Kabelparken (http://copenhagencablepark.squarespace.com; open Apr–mid-Oct); or if you already have the skills, you can use their facilities for 300dkk per hour (including equipment). You can also hire equipment and take kite-surfing lessons with KiteCPH (www.kitecph.dk), based at Amager Strandpark.

A handball match at Brøndby Hallen

ICE-SKATING

Numerous stretches of water within the capital's boundaries freeze up in winter and outdoor rinks *(skøjtebaner)* are set up at Frederiksberg Runddel and Kongens Nytorv. The biggest outdoor ice-skating rink in Northern Europe can be found in Genforeningspladsen, 4km (2.5 miles) northwest of the city centre – skate rental is available daily in winter until 8pm.

ACTIVITY TOURS

If trudging round after an umbrella-waving guide feels too slow, pick up the pace with an activity tour. Running Copenhagen (tel: 20 58 58 77; http://running-copenhagen.dk) has various themed tours, including an interesting route focusing on the city's architecture – you'll need an average running speed of 6 minutes per kilometre if you want to keep up. Running Tours Copenhagen (tel: 50 86 95 04; www.runningtours.dk) visits similar places, and can tailor tours to individuals for a slightly higher price.

In Copenhagen, cycling is more a way of life than a sport. You can easily hire a bicycle (see page 134) and set out on your own, but there are many companies offering guided explorations of the city – try Boom Bike Tours (http://copenhagen-biketours.dk), Cycling Copenhagen (www.cycling-copenhagen.dk) or Bike Copenhagen with Mike (http://bikecopenhagenwithmike.dk). Mountain bikers can head for the purpose-built 26km (16-mile) trail network in Hareskoven woods, 14km (9 miles) northwest of the city, either under their own pedal-power or with a guide from MTB Tours (http://mtb-tours.dk).

SPECTATOR SPORTS

Football
The Danish football team competes at the highest level, and the sport has an enthusiastic following. The main Copenhagen stadium is at Parken (http://parken.dk), and is often used for major international matches. It is also the home ground of F.C. Copenhagen, the most successful club in Danish league football.

Handball
In winter, handball is the country's official game. The successful KIF Kolding København team play at Kolding-Hallen sports arena (www.koldinghallerne.dk) or Brøndby Hallen (www.broendby-hallen. dk), depending on fixtures. Tickets can be purchased from www.billetlugen.dk

Mountain of Rubbish

Denmark is hardly the hilliest of countries; but if you can't go to the mountain, you must bring the mountain to you. An innovative project is currently in plan to build a waste incinerator whose roof will double as a year-round ski slope. Amager Bakke (www.a-r-c.dk) is due for completion in 2017.

HISTORY: KEY DATES

An expanding and contracting economic and political power, Denmark has, in its time, ruled over much of Europe and Scandinavia. It is now an independent-minded member of the EU.

VIKING PERIOD

c.AD 700–1000 The Vikings colonize Britain, Normandy and southern Sweden, and also reach Greenland, Canada, Russia and Constantinople.

960 Harald Bluetooth converts to Christianity.

MIDDLE AGES

1157 Valdemar I unifies Denmark after a century of unrest.

c.1160 Bishop Absalon builds the first castle on Slotsholmen.

1254 Købmandshavn (Copenhagen) receives a charter. The German Hanseatic League recognises its important role in Baltic trade.

1282 Danish nobles force the unpopular king Erik V to sign the Great Charter at Nyborg, limiting his authority.

1340 Accession of Valdemar Atterdag (1340–75) who reinforces royal power and expands its territories.

1397 Margrethe I (1375–1412) sets up the Kalmar Union, an alliance with Norway and Sweden, in which Denmark rules all three.

1417 Erik VII builds Kronborg Castle at Helsingør, a fortress and 'toll booth' to collect money from ships passing through the Sound.

1443 Copenhagen becomes Denmark's capital.

1479 Copenhagen University is founded.

RENAISSANCE

1523 The Kalmar Union ends with Gustav Vasa's coronation as King of Sweden. Norway remains part of Denmark until 1814.

1536 The Reformation: Denmark becomes a Protestant country.

1588–1648 The city expands in the 60-year reign of Christian IV but Denmark's entry (1625–29) into the Thirty Years' War (1618–48) against the

The Øresund bridge links Denmark to Sweden

	Holy Roman Empire is a costly disaster. Further fighting (1643–45) against Swedish forces sees heavy Danish territorial losses.
1658–59	Denmark loses another war with Sweden, ceding a third of its territories, including control over the profitable Sound.
1665	Frederik III establishes an hereditary absolute monarchy.

18TH AND 19TH CENTURIES

1711–12	Plague claims a third of Copenhagen's population.
1728	Major fires gut much of the city leading to reconstruction.
1754	The Royal Danish Academy of Art is founded, inspiring a 'Golden Age' (1800–50) of the arts.
1801–14	Copenhagen is bombarded by the English Navy to prevent her from doing business with France. Britain attacks again in 1807. Denmark sides with France and is bankrupt by 1813. Denmark loses Norway to Sweden in the Treaty of Kiel.
1848–9	Frederik VII abolishes absolute monarchy.
1864	After war with Prussia and Austria, Denmark cedes her territories of Schleswig and Holstein to Germany.

20TH AND 21ST CENTURIES

1914–18	Denmark remains neutral during the First World War.
1929–40	Welfare state is set up under a left-wing coalition dominated by the Social Democrats. Economic depression in the 1930s.
1940–45	Neutral Denmark is invaded by Germany in 1940. It joins the Allies in 1943 and the Resistance takes most of the Jewish population to safety in Sweden. Britain liberates Denmark in 1945.
1968–71	Christiania is founded after student unrest.
1972	Margrethe II becomes queen.
1973	Denmark joins the EEC (EU).
1989	Denmark is the first country to recognise same-sex marriages.
2000	Denmark votes against the euro. The Øresund Bridge, a rail and road link with Sweden, opens.
2011	Helle Thorning-Schmidt, Denmark's first female prime minister, leads a centre-left coalition into power.
2014	Copenhagen Zoo attracts global condemnation when it feeds a young giraffe to its lions.

BEST ROUTES

The Alberto K restaurant

VESTERBRO

This route takes you from Central Station through Vesterbro, Copenhagen's former red-light district. Vesterbro retains its seamier edges, but is also one of the most vibrant parts of the city: Istedgade is full of one-off boutiques, and buzzing cafés, bars and restaurants pack the old butchers' quarter Kødbyen.

> **DISTANCE:** 5km (3 miles)
> **TIME:** A half/full day
> **START:** Hovedbanegården
> **END:** Bakkehuset
> **POINTS TO NOTE:** This is quite a lengthy route. If you want to speed things up and possibly combine with all or part of the Frederiksberg Walk (see page 69), after Værnedamsvej, take a 6A bus down Vesterbrogade to Pile Allé (turn left for Carlsberg) or on to the zoo.

Until the mid-19th century, Vesterbrogade, Vesterbro's main street, was the paved and busy road that led to Copenhagen's west gate, or 'Vesterport', through a country area mainly put to pasture with a few industrial buildings and timber yards. Until 1853, building outside the city walls was not allowed except with express permission. However, with the rise of industrialisation, dreadful sanitation, increased pressure on living space within the city walls and a cholera outbreak in June 1853, which killed around 4,500 people, this prohibition was lifted. In 1856, the city ramparts and gates were pulled down

Vesterbro was never an expensive area and when the red-light district in Pisserenden was cleared out in the early 1900s, many of its workers came to Vesterbro. There is still a red-light district here, but it is contained in a few streets, and the area is better represented by the resident immigrant population and the young artists and designers who also favour the area.

In the past, living conditions here have been poor; it's still a grittier district than some, but gentrification has begun to set in and restoration and improvements have been made. Vesterbro is becoming quite the 'hipster' area and you will come across some quirky, unusual shops and cafés on this route.

OUTSIDE THE STATION

Start outside **Hovedbanegården ❶**, designed in 1911 by the prolific railway architect Heinrich Wenck, who drafted plans for 150 of Denmark's stations. The country's first railway line (built in 1847–8) ran from here to Roskilde (see page

Trendy Vesterbro bar   *Bull sculpture in Kødbyen*

90). Look left, and in the middle of the road you will see an obelisk, the **Freedom Pillar** (Frihedstøtten).

The Freedom Pillar

Unveiled in 1797, when it stood outside the city walls, the Freedom Pillar commemorates the end of adscription in 1788, which meant that peasants could leave the estate where they were born and choose to live and work elsewhere. Before this, they were legally tied to their feudal lord and could be hunted down, brought back and punished severely if they tried to leave. The four figures represent Loyalty, Civic Virtue, Cultivating the Soil and Valour.

Radisson Blu Royal Hotel

The tower block on the corner of Vesterbrogade and Hammerichsgade is the **Radisson Blu Royal Hotel ❷**, an icon in the history of architecture erected in 1960 by Arne Jacobsen (1902–71), the architect/designer, credited with almost single-handedly creating the world's concept of practical but stylish and elegant Danish design. **Room 606** is the only one that retains Jacobsen's original design, but you can admire his famous 'Egg' and 'Swan' chairs in the lobby. The 20th-floor restaurant **Alberto K** provides wonderful evening meals and panoramic views.

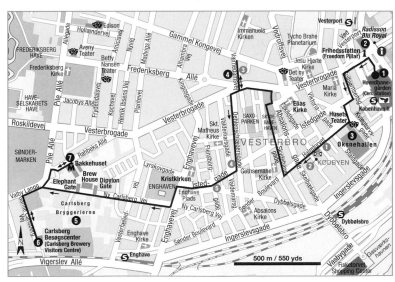

Performance at Øsknehallen

INTO VESTERBRO

Turn left down Vesterbrogade, and left again onto Colbjørnsensgade. You are now in the red-light area. A recent influx of young families and hip bars and restaurants has diluted this notorious district, although you'll still see a few disreputable clubs and interesting window displays. Turn right into Istedgade and left down Helgoslandgade into Halmtorvet, a former haymarket and now home to several cafés. Opposite is **Øksnehallen** ❸ (Halmtorvet 11; charge for exhibitions), an old cattle market now regenerated into a large and lovely tradefair and exhibition space.

Kødbyen

Stretching several blocks to the west is Kødbyen ('Meat Town'), the former butchers' district, which has reinvented itself as one of the most dynamic areas of Copenhagen. The former cattle pens, slaughterhouses and market halls now contain gallery spaces, small, creative companies, and the city's coolest bars, cafés and clubs. Stop here for lunch at one of the many fabulous restaurants, including the all-organic **Bio Mio**, see ❶, or pizza-makers **Mother**, see ❷; or return after sundown to sample the area's lively nightlife.

Continue down Halmtorvet and turn right six streets down into **Skydebane-gade**. Walk past the yellow townhouses and cross the main road. Go through the gate in the imposing brick wall opposite, which leads into **Skydebanehaven**. This park once belonged to the Royal Shooting Club, whose former mansion-like clubhouse, at the far end of the park, was one of the first buildings in Vesterbro. To reach the clubhouse, walk through the kids' play area and follow the path to the exit, turning left onto Absalonsgade, and left again onto Vesterbrogade.

Værnedamsvej

Continue along Vesterbrogade, to the junction with Frederiksberg Allé. Then, turn right up **Værnedamsvej** ❹, famous for its gourmet shopping and a good place for lunch or early supper; try **Les Trois Cochons**, see ❸. Once you've finished exploring this tasty little street, return to Vesterbrogade and then cross the road into Oehlenschlægersgade where you will find, on the corner with Kaalundsgade, an extraordinary mosaic-covered building, reminiscent of Gaudi's work in Barcelona – all lovingly put together by the late Nigerian-born artist Manuel Tafat.

The Carlsberg Brewery

Continue to the end of the street and turn right along Istegade. If you want an afternoon coffee, there are several good cafés along here, notably **Bang and Jensen**, see ❹, and tiny **Riccos**, see ❺, as well as some interesting independent shops. After passing four streets, turn left onto Enghavevej. Keep going and turn right at a large crossroads onto Ny Carlsberg Vej, where you are heading for the **Carlsberg Brewery** ❺ (Carlsberg Bryggerierne). The actual brewing of the world-famous

Inside the Carlsberg Brewery   *Retro Carlsberg poster*

lager takes place in a modern industrial estate in the suburbs, but there are plans to turn the former industrial area into a huge cultural and residential quarter over the next 15 to 20 years.

Head for the archway in the distance. After crossing Væsterfælledvej, look to your left to see the tall **winding chimney** decorated with lotus flowers (hard to see from a distance) and gargoyles (copied from Notre-Dame in Paris). Carlsberg wanted to prove that an industrial chimney could be beautiful so commissioned one of Copenhagen's most celebrated architects, Vilhelm Dahlerup, to design this one in 1900.

The first archway, called the **Dipylon Gate**, was built in 1892 and originally housed two malting floors; malt was loaded in and out of carriages through tubes in the gate's ceiling. The figure group on the roof, by sculptor Stephen Sinding, is called *The Bell Strikers*. The mosaics on the other side of the gate show Carl Jacobsen, his wife Ottilia and son and heir Alf (who died in 1890); Vilhelm Dahlerup and master builder S.P. Beckmann; and four figures representing the brewery's employees.

Go through and you will see another archway held up by the four, famous life-size **Carlsberg elephants**. They were partly inspired by the elephants holding up the organ in Our Saviour's Church (Vor Frelsers Kirke, see page 86) and partly by Bernini's obelisk-carrying elephant in Piazza Minerva in Rome. Note the copper busts of Carl and Ottilia Jacobsen looking down from a gallery at the top of the gate.

The Renaissance-style building on the right of the gate is the Brew House, with a balcony modelled on those in the Palazzo Bavilaque in Verona. On the roof is a large copper sculpture representing *Thor's Battle Against the Giants*. Walk under the 'Elephant Gate' to the end, passing, on your left, the former Carlsberg Museum, now used as a restaurant.

The Carlsberg Visitor Centre

Turn left onto Valby Langgade and then take the first left into Gamle Carlsberg Vej. Halfway down on the left you will find the **Carlsberg Visitor Centre** ❻ (Carlsberg Besøgscenter; Gamle Carlsberg

Carlsberg Beer

The Carlsberg brewery was set up by ale-brewer Jacob Christian Jacobsen (1811–87) in 1847, the year that he produced his first commercial beer using the new German lagering process. He named the brewery after his five-year old son Carl; 'berg' refers to the hill on which it was built. Carl built a second brewery close by in 1882 and took the ancient swastika symbol as the new Carlsberg trademark. Both father and son espoused perfection, Jacobsen *père* even citing it in his will, 'In working the brewery it should be a constant purpose, regardless of immediate gain, to develop the art of making beer to the greatest possible degree of perfection'.

An old cart used to transport beer out of the brewery

Vej 11; www.visitcarlsberg.dk; Tue–Sun 10am–5pm; charge) in buildings which date from 1867. The exhibition offers an interesting insight into brewing past and present and the opportunity to see the dray horses in their stables and, of course, sample a beer.

Bakkehuset

Retrace your steps to the top of Ny Carlsberg Vej, continue down Pile Allé, then take the second right, Rahbeks Allé, to find the oldest building in the area. **Bakkehuset ⑦** (Rahbeks Allé 23; www.bakkehus museet.dk; Tue–Sun 11am–4pm; charge) dates from the 1650s when it was an inn on the road to Copenhagen. From 1787, it was home to Kamma and Knud Lyne Rahbek, literary personalities of the 19th-century Golden Age (see page 58). It is now a cultural museum, furnished in a rather sparse romantic style. The poets Johannes Ewald (1743–81) and Adam Oehlenschläger (1779–1850), are featured heavily (Oehlenschläger was the Rahbeks' son-in-law) and there is also memorabilia relating to Hans Christian Andersen (1805–75; see page 56), who came here often in his youth.

To save yourself a long walk home, continue down Rahbeks Allé to Vesterbrogade and take the 6A bus back into town.

Food and Drink

❶ BIO MIO
Halmtorvet 19; tel: 33 31 20 00; http://biomio.dk; daily noon–11pm; €
Organic, self-service canteen, whose super-fresh dishes are ordered directly with the chef then consumed at communal tables.

❷ MOTHER
Høkerboderne 9–15; tel: 22 27 58 98; http://mother.dk; Mon–Sat 11am–11pm, Sun 11am–10pm; €
One of the city's favourite pizza places thanks to its cosy atmosphere and small, select menu of sourdough creations.

❸ LES TROIS COCHONS
Værnedamsvej 10; tel: 33 31 70 55; www.cofoco.dk; Mon–Sat noon–2.30pm, daily 5.30pm–10pm; €
This atmospheric, elegant old butcher's shop delivers both style and good food (in the form of a three-course set menu) at a very good price.

❹ BANG AND JENSEN
Istedgade 130; tel: 33 25 53 18; http://blog.bangogjensen.dk; Mon–Fri 7.30am–2am, Sat 10am–2am, Sun 10am–midnight, kitchen closes at 10pm daily; €
A former pharmacy, now a cool and very popular café-bar. Particularly good brunches.

❺ RICCOS
Istedgade 119; tel: 31 21 04 40; daily 9am–11pm; €
Tiny coffee house that does excellent coffee.

Fashionable Strøget

THE OLD INNER CITY

This circular walk takes you through the oldest part of Copenhagen and encompasses Strøget, Copenhagen's long 'walking street', Gammel Strand (Old Beach) and the University or Latin Quarter. It is now a very lively area full of shops, bars and restaurants.

DISTANCE: 3.5km (2 miles)
TIME: A half/full day
START/END: Rådhuspladsen
POINTS TO NOTE: This walk takes quite a while if you visit everything. However, if you want to combine part of it with other walks, from Højbro Plads you can visit Slotsholmen (see page 78) or continue down Strøget to Kongens Nytorv and Nyhavn (see pages 43 and 45).

With the exception of Slotsholmen (see page 78), this is the oldest part of Copenhagen. Predominantly built in wood, the old city was a martyr to fire and almost completely demolished in 1728 and 1795. The first fire destroyed nearly 50 percent of the medieval city and made 20 percent of the population homeless; the second pretty much finished off the job. So, although the area has been inhabited for over 700 years, there are very few buildings that remain from before the 18th century.

Start at Rådhuspladsen (see page 76), which was built in the 19th cen-

tury just inside the old city walls (now demolished) and walk down Frederiks-berggade, one of the five streets that make up **Strøget** (literally 'stripe' and pronounced 'stroll'), the world's longest pedestrianised street, which reaches all the way to royal Kongens Nytorv (see page 43) by the harbour.

This western end of Strøget is the least sophisticated part, characterised by fast-food joints and cheap fashion stores, in contrast with the middle and final stretches, where you will find Danish design and top fashion brands.

GAMMELTORV

Follow the cobbles to the first large open area that you come to. This is the site of Havn, Copenhagen's oldest village. **Gammeltorv ❶** (Old Square), on your left, is the city's oldest meeting place where, in the Middle Ages, everything took place; a little like Rådhuspladsen today.

Gammeltorv suffered in both fires and the town hall that had stood facing inwards on what is now the intersection with **Nytorv ❷** (New Square) was burnt

The old city rooftops

down on both occasions. Rebuilt in the same place after 1728, after the second fire it was rebuilt on Nytorv in the hope that the space created would act as a windbreak in the event of another fire. You can see its old outline in pale stone where the fruit-and-vegetable market usually stands.

On your left, you will see the **Caritas Fountain** (Springvandet). This is Copenhagen's oldest external water supply and is linked by pipes to a water source 6km (4 miles) away. It was a gift to the city in 1608 from Christian IV: the pregnant, lactating woman with her two children represents *Caritas* (Charity). The fountain becomes

extra glitzy on important royal birthdays, when it is filled with golden apples.

The curved facade of **Stellings Hus**, designed by Arne Jacobsen (who also designed the Radisson Blu Royal Hotel (see page 29), stands nearby on the corner of Skindergade.

NYTORV

On your right is where the gallows used to stand on Nytorv. The executions that took place here were well attended and provided locals with a macabre form of entertainment. Between 1720 and 1730 there were 14 executions;

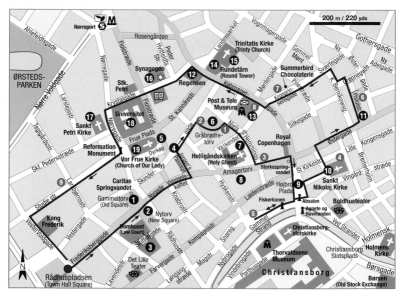

Statue on Kobmagergade   *Gråbrødretorv is a delightful café square*

sadly, most of them were impoverished women driven to killing their newborn babies. The last execution, of two counterfeiters, took place in 1758, while branding and whipping continued until the late 1780s. The outline of the paler stones on Nytorv shows the position of the whipping post.

On the right-hand side, on the former site of the Royal Orphanage, which burnt down in the fire of 1728, you will find the classical porticoed grandeur of **Domhuset**, the third town hall. This was built by the architect C.F. Hansen between 1805–15 (with a delay in 1807 when the British bombarded the city); Hansen was also responsible for rebuilding the cathedral, Church of Our Lady (see page 41). Domhuset was the town hall until 1905 when, owing to space issues, a new one was built on Rådhuspladsen (Town Hall Square). It is still used as Copenhagen's main Law Court (hence the large inscription above the ionic columns, "By law shall the land be built") and is the largest in Denmark. On its far side, on **Slutterigade ❸** (Prison Street), you can see the two enclosed bridges that linked the courthouse to the prison.

INTO THE LATIN QUARTER

Carry on down Strøget until you reach the crossroads of Knabrostræde and Skoubogade – take a left for chocolate heaven at **PB Chokolade** or enjoy coffee and cake at **La Glace**. Otherwise, continue until you see a sign for **Jorgen's**

Passage ❹ on your left, an appealing arcade with some good kids' and home decor shops. Walk through to the end. Opposite is **Fiolstræde ❺** – in the centre of the Latin Quarter around the university – with a few pretty outdoor restaurants and the back of the Church of Our Lady (Vor Frue Kirke). To experience something of the studious atmosphere, visit the excellent antiquarian/second-hand bookshop at 34–36 or grab a coffee at the library-like book café at 10–12.

Gråbrødretorv

Turn right down Skindergade (Hide Street), originally home to furriers and tanners, and walk through to **Gråbrødretorv ❻**

Streets off Strøget

Although this walk takes in the major sights, don't be afraid to wander down streets that take your fancy; there are many treasures (historical and retail) around almost every corner. Unexpected finds are part of the pleasure of ambling around this area. North and south of Strøget, the streets offer more individual shopping in little one-off boutiques, record and second-hand shops. Streets to head for include Skindergade, Larsbjørnstræde and the three parallel streets: Vestergade, Studiestræde, Sankt Peders Stræde; and Læderstræde and Kompagnistræde, which run into each other; the latter is especially good for antiques shops.

Colourful Skindergade houses

(Grey Brothers Square), a delightful square named after the grey-clad monks who lived here from 1238 in Copenhagen's first monastery. The monks were turned out just before the Reformation in 1536, and the monastery became a hospital. Many of the houses here date from after the fire of 1728 and are known as 'fire houses', a gabled, brick-built design that was introduced in the hope that it would be more fire-safe than the medieval timbered buildings that burnt so easily.

Fire Damage

The terrible fire of 1728 raged for three days, destroying much of medieval Copenhagen. Surprisingly, when the flames died down, plans to rebuild the city in a more fireproof style were met with widespread opposition. Very few of the streets were widened – people were loath to lose their land to roadways – and although some narrow 'fire houses' were built, much of the construction was done in wood, as it was cheaper than brick.

After a second conflagration in 1795, the construction of houses in brick was enforced, and terraces had to have oblique corners to enable fire engines to get around more easily, thus creating small octagonal squares all over the city. Styles changed and unadorned neoclassical facades, without balconies, became popular.

The second fire of 1795 destroyed much of the rebuild – the style that followed was plainer and more classical. The square is now filled with restaurants and is a pleasant place to eat out in summer. **Peder Oxe**, see ①, or **Sporvejen**, see ②, are good options if you are already thinking about lunch.

Church of the Holy Ghost

Cross the square and then take a right onto Niels Hemmingsensgade. The church here is the **Church of the Holy Ghost** ❼ (Helligåndskirken; Niels Hemmingsensgade 5; www.helligaandskirken.dk; Mon–Fri noon–4pm; Sunday service 10am).

A hospice stood on this site as early as 1296. It was incorporated into the monastery in 1474. Most of the church, including the bells that were given by Christian IV in 1647, was destroyed in 1728. Even the coffins under the floor were destroyed. What survived the fire – **Helligåndshuset** (now used for markets and exhibitions); **Christian IV's impressive** main door, made in 1630 and originally intended for the Stock Exchange (see page 79); and **Griffenfeld's Chapel** (the round burial chapel on the north side) – constitute some of the oldest architectural remains in Copenhagen. The church was reopened in 1732. Admirers of the philosopher Søren Kirkegaard might like to note that it was here that he first saw Régine, the girl to whom he became engaged, but whom he subsequently rejected.

Modern glassware　　　　　　　　　　　*The Royal Café*

AMAGERTORV

Turn left out of the church back onto Strøget and you are almost immediately on **Amagertorv** ❽, another square punctuating the 1.5km (1-mile) length of Strøget. From here on, the shopping on Strøget becomes infinitely smarter.

Georg Jensen, Royal Copenhagen and Stork Fountain

To your left you will find two great Danish design institutions, the silversmith **Georg Jensen** (Amagertorv 4; www.georgjensen.com; Mon–Fri 10am–7pm, Sat 10am–6pm, Sun 10am–4pm; free) and **Royal Copenhagen** (Amagertorv 6; www.royalcopenhagen.com; Mon–Sat 10am–6pm, Sun 11am–5pm; free), the hand-painted porcelain manufacturer. They are housed side by side in two ornate, rather lovely Renaissance buildings, built for wealthy merchants.

Next door is **Illums Bolighus**, a furniture design mecca (see page 18) and ahead of you, the **Stork Fountain**, Storkespringvandet, erected in 1894 to mark the silver wedding of Crown Prince Frederik (VIII) and his wife, Princess Louise. It's a popular meeting place, and also where newly-qualified Danish midwives come for a celebratory dance!

If you are in need of a drink or a bite to eat, two good places spring to mind: the powder-puff-pink **Royal Smushi Café**, see ❸, or the charming **Restaurant Maven**, see ❹, a short walk away at the Church of St Nicholas.

HØJBRO PLADS

From here, turn right into **Højbro Plads** ❾, home to a dramatic equestrian statue of Copenhagen's founder, Bishop Absalon. It dates from 1901 and is the work of Danish sculptors Christian Gottlieb Vilhelm Bissen, who cast the figure, and Martin Nyrop, who was responsible for the plinth. Walk down and, to your right, you will find **Gammel Strand** (Old Beach) where, from early days, fishermen used to bring in their herring catches and their wives (the 'fishwives') sold them. **Fiskerko-**

Royal Copenhagen

Royal Copenhagen, the Danish manufacturer of handmade and hand-painted porcelain, was founded in 1775 by Frantz Müller, a chemist who had succeeded in mastering the difficult art of Chinese-style hard-paste porcelain. Its first designs – 'Blue Fluted', dating from 1775, based on Chinese floral motifs and 'Blue Flower', which is a little more naturalistic and dates from 1779 – were in cobalt blue, the only colour to withstand the high firing temperatures required. Its most ambitious design, 'Flora Danica', shows copies of botanical drawings and was originally commissioned by the king for Catherine the Great in 1790. The 1,802 pieces in the range took 12 years for one artist to paint. All three designs are still in production today.

Statue of Bishop Absalon

nen, a statue of a sturdy fishwife by Christian Svejstrup Madsen, dates from 1940 and usually stands on the corner of the steps down to the canal that still separates the Old Town from Slotsholmen (see page 78); however, she had been temporarily removed at the time of writing because of the building of the new Gammel Strand metro station (due for completion in 2018).

If you are hungry for a solid, proper, delicious lunch, one of the city's most renowned fish restaurants, **Krogs**, see ⑤, is located on Gammel Strand. On the other side of the canal, the porticoed building is the palace church, **Christiansborg Slotskirke** (see page 80) and to the right of that, the ochre building is the **Thorvaldsen's Museum** (see page 81). Looking ahead and to the left from the statue of Absalon, the copper roofs and twisting spire belong to the Renaissance **Børsen**, the old Stock Exchange (see page 79). The spire to the left is **Holmens Kirke**, the old navy church (see page 79).

Before turning back, cross to the middle of the bridge and look over the left side down to the water where you will see eight figures with their hands outstretched pleadingly beneath the surface. This little-known figure group, by sculptor Suste Bonnén, depicts part of the legend of **Agnete and the Merman**, a story in which peasant girl Agnete marries a merman and has seven sons but then fails to return after visiting her home village.

CHURCH OF ST NICHOLAS

Walk back up towards Strøget and take a right down Lille Kirkestræde to the **Church of St Nicholas** ⑩ (Sankt Nikolaj Kirke; Nikolaj Plads 10; www.nikolaj kunsthal.dk; Tue–Wed and Fri–Sun noon–5pm, Thu noon–9pm; charge, free Wed), named after the patron saint of sailors – an apt sponsor in a seaboard town. The mother church of the Reformation in 1536, it survived the 1728 fire, but was not so lucky in 1795 when everything but the tower was razed to the ground. Rebuilt in rather imposing red brick in the early 20th century, it is now an exhibition hall for modern art.

ON TO KØBMAGERGADE

Cross over Store Kirkestraede back onto Strøget. Turn right down to Kristen Bernikows Gade and cross the road. To your right you will see the back of Magasin du Nord (see page 44) and a small flower market. Continue until you reach a sign-posted archway for **Pistolstræde** ⑪. Walk to the end, past various smart shops, until you reach the little courtyard with **L'Alsace**, see ⑥ (which has hosted Pope John Paul II and Elton John no less), where you will see the timbered backs of 17th-century houses; unusual in an Old Town that has succumbed to two major fires.

Walk through to Grønnegade, a pretty street (look at the houses to

Folk musicians
Post & Tele Museum

your right) and turn left, then right back on to Kristen Bernikows Gade. Take the first left on to Sværtergade: the little yellow building on the right, constructed immediately after the first fire, is the smallest house in the old town. One block further, Sværtergade turns into Kronprinsensgade, one of Copenhagen's poshest shopping streets (even if it does have a 7/11 on the corner). **Summerbird Chocolaterie** (Kronprinsensgade 11; Mon–Thu 10am–6pm, Fri 10am–7pm, Sat 10am–4pm), another well-known chocolate maker, can be found along here, as can Copenhagen's oldest tea-shop, **A.C. Perch Thehandel**, see ❼, at No. 5.

At the end, turn right onto Købmagergade. Opposite you is the **Post & Tele Museum** and further down on your right, the **Round Tower**; **Trinity Church** next to it; and, opposite, **Regensen** ⓬, a 17th-century student hall of residence, which is still in use.

Post & Tele Museum

Copenhagen's main post office is home to the **Post & Tele Museum** ⓭ (Købmagergade 37; tel: 33 41 09 00; www.ptt-museum.dk; daily 10am–4pm; free), which charts the history of communication from the 17th century. Even though labelling is mostly in Danish, it makes for an interesting browse. Ignore the stamp collection and head up to **Café Hovedtelegrafen** for excellent views, see ❽.

Round Tower

Continue down Købmagergade until you see the **Round Tower** (Rundetårn) ⓮ (Kobmagergade 52a; tel: 33 73 03 73; www.rundetaarn.dk; mid-May–mid-Sept: daily 10am–8pm; rest of year Tue & Wed 10am–9pm, Thu–Mon 10am–6pm; charge), the round red-brick tower on your right. This unusual building is a 17th-century observatory, the oldest in Europe, and was used by astronomers at the University of Copenhagen until 1861. It was the tallest building in Copenhagen when Christian IV had it built, and is thought to be mentioned in H.C. Andersen's fairytale of the *Soldier and the Tinder Box* where a dog is described as having 'eyes as big as a tower'. Andersen knew this tower well and, as an observatory, it was literally an 'eye' on the heavens.

Inside, a wide cobbled ramp spirals up through the tower, designed for a horse and cart to transport heavy equipment all the way to the top. In 1716, Tsar Peter of Russia himself galloped his horse to the top of the 209-metre (686ft) ramp inside the Round Tower, followed more sedately by his wife in a carriage. Now there is a yearly unicycle race to the top and back, usually held in May. There is also an art gallery, formerly the university library, about half way up.

Trinity Church

Next door is **Trinity Church** ⓯ (Trinitatis Kirke; Købmagergade 52a/Landemærket 12; www.trinitatiskirke.dk; Mon–Sat 9.30am–4.30pm), commissioned

The main post office building

as the university church by Christian IV, and finished in 1657 under Frederik III.

Although the Round Tower survived the blaze of 1728, the church suffered. Its roof and the university library that lay beneath it were charred to a crisp and its interior damaged. But it was quickly restored by 1731 and is now a lovely white-and-gold Rococo affair with a splendid Baroque altarpiece, a three-faced Rococo clock, a vaulted roof picked out in gold, galleries running down both side walls and a fabulous gold- and silver-coloured organ. If it is open, it is worth a visit; otherwise, look down the nave through a glass panel as you start up the Round Tower.

KRYSTALGADE

Continue and turn left up Krystalgade, the spire of the Church of Our Lady (Vor Frue Kirke) in view. The large red-brick building set behind grey railings a little way up on your right is Copenhagen's **Grand Synagogue** ⑯ (Synagogen; usually closed to the public). The centre for Judaism in Denmark, it dates from 1883 and, amazingly, survived the Nazi occupation. Its interior is notable for Egyptian-influenced elements. Its sacred Torah scrolls were hidden in Trinity Church during World War II.

Cross over Filostræde. The back of the university building is on your left (you can see the book stacks through the windows) and the **Hotel Sankt Petri**, where you can settle down for an early evening cocktail, is a little further up, also on your right.

NØRREGADE

At the end of the street, take a left onto Nørregade. On your right is the **Church of St Peter** ⑰.

Church of St Peter

The first Church of St Peter (Sankt Petri Kirke; Larslejsstæde 11; Apr–Sept: Wed–Sat 11am–3pm) was built here in around 1200 in the Romanesque style. It burnt down and was replaced, c.1450, with a Gothic structure, minus the transepts, which were added in the 17th century.

During the Reformation, the church was deconsecrated and turned into a canon foundry, but in 1585 it was reinstated and given to the German-speaking population by Frederik II. German was the main language spoken by the court and, as a result, Sankt Petri became an important intellectual, economic and political meeting place.

The fire of 1728 destroyed its interior, and new decoration, including the Baroque main entrance (1730s) and the copper-clad spire (1757), were introduced. Its vaulted sepulchral chapel (1681–83), which has some impressive statuary, is the resting place of the royal architect Nicolai Eigtved (1701–54), who designed the church spire; and possibly of the German doctor Johann Struensee (1737–72), who stepped into the king's shoes and ruled Denmark for over a year before being imprisoned in Kastellet and executed.

The Absolut Icebar at Hotel 27　　　　　*The café at the Hotel Sankt Petri*

The University

On your left, as you walk towards the Church of Our Lady, there is a square. The building facing the side of the church is the **University** ⑱ (Universitet). There has been a university in Copenhagen since 1479 and it currently educates around 37,000 students. It was located on the corner of Nørregade and Studiestræde until just after the Reformation in 1536, when it was moved across the street to the vacated Bishops Palace.

The fires of 1728 and 1795 and the British Navy bombardment in 1807 destroyed many buildings; the current one dates from the 19th century. The portrait busts are of illustrious professors.

Church of Our Lady

Copenhagen's cathedral, the **Church of Our Lady** ⑲ (Vor Frue Kirke; Nørregade, Vor Frue Plads; http://koebenhavnsdom kirke.dk; daily 8am–5pm) is the latest in a long line of church buildings, dating back to 1209, to stand on this spot. Fires destroyed two of the earlier churches, and the current building was built to replace the one destroyed by the British bombardment of 1807, when the navy used the church spire as a target. Designed by C.F. Hansen, it dates from 1829: only the tower and the walls of the side aisles remain of the medieval building. The front door is guarded by towering statues of **King David** and **Moses**, while the interior is noteworthy for its reliefs and imposing marble statues by Bertel Thorvaldsen (see page 81), dating from 1839. These include **Christ and the 12 Apostles** (with Judas replaced by St Paul) on the altar and along the side walls; and the beautiful angel holding a shell, which serves as the cathedral's font. Two of its four bells have claims to fame: one, dating to 1490, is the oldest in the country; while 'Stormklokken' is the heaviest bell in Denmark, weighing a hefty four tons.

Outside the cathedral, the **monument** on Bispetorvet commemorates the 400th anniversary of the Reformation. Cross the square and head down Studiestræde opposite the Church of Our Lady, past **The Living Room**, see ⑨. Take a left at the next junction and a short walk will bring you back to Rådhuspladsen.

Royal Weddings

When Crown Prince Frederik married Australian commoner Mary Donaldson in May 2004, walking her down the aisle of the Church of Our Lady (Vor Frue Kirke), he was following in the footsteps of some of his forebears: Queen Margrethe I who, at the age of nine, married the Norwegian king Haakan in 1363; and Christian I who married his queen, Dorothea, here in 1449. The Danish monarchy holds the record for unbroken succession from the Viking chief Gorm the Old, father of Harald Bluetooth, who died in c.958, of fifty kings (predominantly named Frederik or Christian) and two queens, both Margrethe – the second celebrated her 40th Jubilee in 2012.

The great organ in the Church of Our Lady

Food and Drink

❶ PEDER OXE
Gråbrødretorv 11; tel: 33 11 00 77; www.pederoxe.dk; 11.30am–10.30pm; €€
This friendly place offers everything from a light lunch to a full three-course meal. Emphasis on fresh organic produce.

❷ SPORVEJEN
Grabrødretorv 17; www.sporvejen.dk; Mon–Sat 11am–10pm, Sun noon–10pm; €
Cheap and cheerful fare (omelettes, burgers etc) in an old Copenhagen tram. Sit out on the square in summer.

❸ THE ROYAL SMUSHI CAFE
Amagertorv 6; www.royalcafe.dk; Mon–Sat 10am–7pm, Sun 10am–6pm; €–€€
Café with courtyard set in a Renaissance building. All dishes are served on Royal Copenhagen porcelain. 'Smushi' (sushi-inspired *smørrebrød*) is a speciality.

❹ RESTAURANT MAVEN
Nikolaj Plads 12; tel: 32 20 11 00; www.restaurantmaven.dk; kitchen Mon–Sat 11.30am–3.30pm and 5.30pm–10pm, also opens for lunch on Sun in July; €€
This acclaimed bistro serves well-presented French-Danish food in a delightfully romantic setting inside a former church.

❺ KROGS FISKERESTAURANT
Gammel Strand 38; tel: 33 15 89 15; www.krogs.dk; Mon–Sat noon–3pm and 6–10pm; €€€€
Booking is essential if you wish to dine at Copenhagen's oldest fish restaurant. The three-course evening menu starts at 345dkk.

❻ L'ALSACE
Ny Østergade 9; tel: 33 14 57 43; www.alsace. dk; Mon–Sat 11.30am–midnight; €–€€€€
Gourmet food from Continental Europe, specialising in Alsace. The three-course lunch menu is good value.

❼ A.C. PERCH THEHANDEL
Kronprinsessgade 5; tel: 33 15 35 62; www.perchstearoom.dk; Mon–Fri 11.30am–5.30pm, Sat 11am–5pm; €€
This teashop has barely changed since 1835 and it offers an astonishing variety of teas. There's also a deliciously tea-centric café on the first floor.

❽ CAFE HOVEDTELEGRAFEN
Købmagergade 37; tel: 33 41 09 86; www.cafehovedtelgrafen.dk; daily 10am–4pm, kitchen shuts an hour earlier; €
This rooftop café offers an airy interior and an outdoor terrace overlooking the rooftops of the old town. Snacks and main meals (mainly fish) are good.

❾ THE LIVING ROOM
Larsbjørnsstræde 17; tel: 33 32 66 10; Mon–Thu 10am–11pm, Fri 10am–1am, Sat 11am–2am, Sun noon–7pm; €
This café-bar on two floors serves a wide range of coffees.

Romantic Kongens Nytorv

THE HARBOUR AREA

This walk is a short but colourful one, starting in Kongens Nytorv (King's New Square), the height of 17th-century aristocratic elegance, and leading down to Nyhavn. Once known for its brothels and seedy taverns, today the harbour is a popular outdoor area with lots of attractive restaurants and bars.

DISTANCE: 1km (0.5 miles)
TIME: 1hr (plus boat trip 1hr)
START: Hôtel d'Angleterre
END: Nyhavn
POINTS TO NOTE: If you don't take a harbour cruise, this is a nice walk to do at the end of the day, ending on Nyhavn for a drink or dinner. If you walk up one of the side streets onto Sankt Annae Plads, it connects easily with the walk of the Royal District (see page 47).

In the Middle Ages, Kongens Nytorv, an elegant square that now seems integral to Copenhagen, was outside the city walls and quite a way from the banks of the Sound. It began to develop under Frederik III (1648–70). In 1671–73, his son Christian V (1670–99) commissioned a canal (now called Nyhavn, or 'New Harbour') to be dug from the Sound to the square so that merchant ships could sail inland and unload their cargo more easily. He also ordered landowners with property bordering on the square to build grand mansions or to sell their land to someone who would.

KONGENS NYTORV

Standing at the bottom of **Strøget** (see page 35) you face Kongens Nytorv with Nyhavn (out of sight) lying on the far side of the square. The metro station is currently being extended to make Kongens Nytorv an interchange for the new Cityringen metro line, hence the building work that you can see. During the pre-construction phase, archaeologists discovered the East Gate of the 11th-century city here. To your left, at the corner of the square is Copenhagen's swankiest hotel, the **Hôtel d'Angleterre**; to your right the building with the fancy cupola is **Magasin du Nord**, the city's oldest department store.

Hôtel d'Angleterre

The **Hôtel d'Angleterre** ❶ has seen its fair share of wealthy visitors since opening its doors in 1755. Guests have included H.C. Andersen, Grace Kelly, Winston Churchill, Margaret Thatcher,

Kunsthal Charlottenborg exhibit

Bill Clinton, Woody Allen, Pierce Brosnan and Madonna. When Michael Jackson stayed in the 1980s, he was so enthralled by some of its furnishings that he wanted to buy them; when politely told they were not for sale, he offered to buy the entire hotel instead. Oddly enough, they declined.

Magasin du Nord

Originally a hotel, the **Magasin du Nord** ❷ dates from the 19th century. At Vingårdstræde 6 is an attic room where Hans Christian Andersen lived while he was studying for his exams in 1827. The department store is also a good stop for a coffee or bite to eat in an area where you pay for the location.

The Royal Theatre and Kunsthal Charlottenborg

The **Royal Theatre** ❸ (Det Kongelige Teater; see page 20) stands opposite the Magasin du Nord on the south side of the square. There has been a theatre here since 1748; the present theatre was built in the 1870s, taking the classically inspired Parisian Opera as its model. It has been somewhat eclipsed by the strikingly modern Royal Danish Playhouse (see page 20). Pop down August Bournonvilles Passage, to the side of the theatre, to see the 1930s mosaic ceiling in the archway.

East of the theatre is **Kunsthal Charlottenborg** ❹ (www.kunsthalcharlottenborg.dk; Tue–Sun 11am–5pm, Wed until 8pm; charge), built in the 17th century as

a palatial residence for Frederik III's illegitimate son Ulrik. Less than a century later, it became the Royal Danish Academy of Fine Arts, where painters, sculptors and architects learned their trade. It is now used for contemporary art exhibitions.

Equestrian Statue of Christian V

Look to the centre of the square where you will see a large **equestrian statue of Christian V** ❺ dressed as a Roman emperor, riding over the fallen figure of Envy. The king is surrounded by Queen Artemisia, Alexander the Great, the goddess Pallas Athene and Hercules. Sculpted by the Frenchman Abraham César Lamoureux, it was the first equestrian statue in Scandinavia and was originally made of gilded lead because bronze castings of this size were not possible at the time. It has been repaired many times and in 1946 was recast in bronze. The original can now be found in Christian IV's Brewery (Bryghus; see page 83).

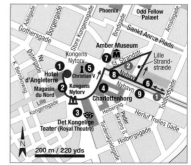

Picturesque Nyhavn   *The Royal Theatre*

NYHAVN

At the bottom of Kongens Nytorv lies the 'New Harbour' or **Nyhavn ❻**, lined with pastel-coloured merchants' houses that date from when the canal was constructed. Their warehouses stood at the end; a couple still survive and are now smart, boutique hotels, The Admiral and 71 Nyhavn (see page 108).

With its attractive historical ships at anchor, Nyhavn is not just of interest for its 17th- and 18th-century mariners' past. From the 1880s, it was also the gateway to a new life in the US, since it was here that you bought your ticket from one of the many shipping offices that sprang up. A new start for many, although not for the 14 unfortunates who set sail to join the Titanic's maiden voyage in 1912, of whom only two survived.

The entrance to Nyhavn is heralded by a large **anchor**, honouring 1,600 Danish sailors who lost their lives in World War II. To the left as you face the Sound is the **Amber Museum ❼** (Kongens Nytorv 2; tel: 33 11 67 00; www.houseofamber. com; Oct–Apr: daily 10am–5.30pm, May–Sept: daily 10am–6.30pm; charge) showcasing Denmark's national gemstone. When you learn that most amber deposits weigh 10g (0.5oz) or less each, you will understand the wonder of the chunk weighing a record-breaking 8.8kg (19lbs 6oz) that they have on display.

Hans Christian Andersen spent around 22 years lodging at various addresses in Nyhavn, because it was close to the Royal Theatre, which he loved. He wrote his first fairytales, including *The Tinder Box* and *The Princess and the Pea*, on the 'shady side' of the canal at **No. 20** (then 289) – such a cold house that in winter his landlady's children poured water on the floor to make ice slides. He also lived for twenty years at **No. 67** on the 'sunny side', and ended his days at **No. 18**.

Nyhavn's North Side

This sunny side of the canal is a popular restaurant area; sit inside or out (blankets and heaters are provided in winter), but grab a seat while you can, as it is almost always busy. The restaurants are all in old buildings and have names such as Skipperkroen (the Skipper's Inn), **Cap Horn**, see ❶, or La Sirène (the Siren); they are linked to the lives and travels of the sailors who used to saunter along here looking for women, drink, a bed and possibly a fight.

Side Streets

The side streets off Nyhavn are well worth a look and, like the harbour itself, have come up in the world. The first turning on your left takes you up **Store Strandstræde** (Big Beach Street), the only remnant of its seafaring past is a tattoo parlour that claims to have been on the site since the 16th century. There's a nice little restaurant called **Zeleste**, see ❷, along here – you'll recognise it by the kitsch, plastic crayfish hanging outside.

Continue along and at the end turn right, back on yourself, down **Lille Strandstræde** (Little Beach Street),

View of the harbour

also home to small galleries and clothes shops. Carry on to the end and you will find yourself back on Nyhavn.

Boat Trips Round the Harbour

If you want to take a boat trip through the harbour area, which is highly recommended, you will find the **Strömma** (Gray Line; www.stromma.dk) tour boats ❽ at the top of Nyhavn near the anchor, and the **Netto Bådene** (www.netto-baadene.dk) boats ❾ further along the south side of the canal. The blue-and-yellow local transport boats also stop at the jetty at the end of Nyhavn. Seeing the city from the water is a great way to understand the layout of this waterside city, which began on the island of Slotsholmen.

On such a trip, you would expect to go up the harbour, passing by the Royal Danish Playhouse (see page 20); the **Opera House** (see page 88); and **Langelinie**, **Kastellet** and *The Little Mermaid* (see page 51). Some tours head further out to **Trekroner**, an 18th-century fort used once in 1801 against the British, before turning back to sail past **Christianshavn** (see page 84), down the **Frederiksberg Kanal**, then past **Slotsholmen** (see page 78) and the royal palace, the **Bryghus**, the **Black Diamond** and **Holmens Kirke**, and back to Nyhavn.

Food and Drink

❶ CAP HORN

Nyhavn 21; tel: 33 12 85 04; www.caphorn.dk; daily 9am–midnight, kitchen open until 11pm; €€

Nyhavn eateries are more about people-watching than food, but this place serves good grub too, including lamb, deer and duck dishes, and some lighter fish mains.

❷ ZELESTE

Store Strandstraede 6; tel: 33 16 06 06; daily 10am–11pm; kitchen open 10.30am–9.30pm; www.zeleste.dk; €-€€

Pretty whitewashed restaurant with cobbled courtyard. Hearty menu changes regularly. Great brunches. Book to avoid disappointment.

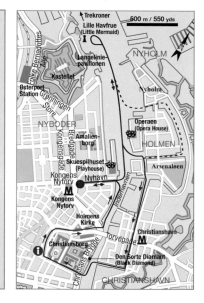

Sankt Annæ Plads at dusk

THE ROYAL DISTRICT

This walk takes you through Copenhagen's grandest quarter, Frederiksstaden, and then along the banks of the Sound. Once a heaving commercial and naval area, its quiet streets are now frequented by tourists and locals, including the royal family, who live at Amalienborg palace at its heart.

DISTANCE: 4km (2.5 miles)
TIME: A half day
START: Sankt Annæ Plads
END: Kongens Nytorv
POINTS TO NOTE: Most of the food options are towards the end of the walk near Bredgade, which makes this a good choice for a morning walk. Alternatively, have a picnic by the Sound or in Kastellet.

In 1749, Frederik V laid the foundation stone for his building project, Frederiksstad, a grand court district adorned with a large and beautiful church rivalling almost anything else in Europe. He was an absolute monarch, belonging to the 300-year-old Oldenburg dynasty, and wanted to create something startling. He even got his wealthy subjects to pay for it. The rococo palaces of the Amalienborg were designed in the 1750s by royal architect Nicolai Eigtved. Several decades later, the royal family moved in, and Amalienborg is still their winter home.

Start at **Sankt Annæ Plads ❶**, a tree-lined boulevard created during the build-ing of Frederiksstaden, when a former canal was filled in. A large **equestrian statue of Christian X** (1912–47) presides over the top end of the 'square', while the harbour end is dominated by the Royal Danish Playhouse (see page 20). Close to the statue is the **Garrison's Church ❷** (Garnisons Kirke; Tue–Fri 9am–1pm; free) and its graveyard, built to replace the castle chapel that burned down in 1689. Copenhagen's garrison attended church here from 1706. The plain white interior is composed of unusual two-storey galleries, with a dramatic black altarpiece (1724) providing the main focus of attention.

AMALIENBORG

From here, cross the square and turn left up **Amaliegade**. Before he became a 'Prince of Denmark' in 1852, at the age of 34, Christian IX lived with his family in a yellow town house at Amaliegade 18, where four of his children were born. Today it is still an exclusive street. There are several embassies along here and the buildings are some of the most elegant

Amalienborg Castle

and expensive in the city. If you need a bite to eat check out **Restaurant Amalie**, see ❶, or the equally popular **Café Toldboden**, see ❷. Go through the arch that leads into the grandest part of Frederiksstad, the square around which the four palaces of **Amalienborg** ❸ stand.

The Palaces

The palace complex Amalienborg was built on the site of a previous palace which burned down in a horrific fire: during a theatrical performance on 19 April 1689 for Christian V's birthday, part of the stage set caught alight and 180 people died in the blaze.

In 1794, the royal family moved in after a fire at Slotsholmen (see page 78), and liked their new home so much that the king purchased all four buildings. They have lived here ever since, members often occupying each palace at different times.

As you stand in the centre of the octagonal 'square' looking back at the colonnade, the palace to your right is **Christian VII's palace** ❹

(Christian VII's Palæ; tours by arrangement only, tel: 33 92 64 92), one of the

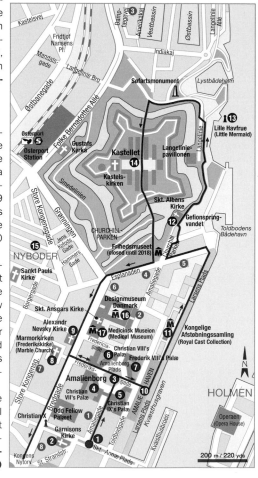

| *Standing guard* | *Christian VIII's Palace* |

first to be finished before Eigtved died in 1754. This was originally the sumptuous home of Lord High Steward Adam Gottlob Moltke and the most expensive of the four; it is widely considered to be Denmark's best rococo interior. Christian VII, who suffered from mental illness for much of his reign, lived here from December 1794 until his death in 1808. The queen now uses it to welcome foreign dignitaries.

On the left of the colonnade, which connects the two palaces, you'll find **Christian IX's Palace** ❺ (Christian IX's Palæ), which is home to Queen Margrethe and Prince Henrik, and was originally known as Schack's Palace. Crown Prince Frederik VI and his wife Marie were the first Royals to move in and lived here for over 40 years. Frederik was Regent and ruled for his father from 1784–1808. Even so, he often needed his father's signature for affairs of state, so he had the colonnade built between the two palaces, with a corridor running through it for easy access.

Turn your back on these palaces and the palace on your left is **Christian VIII's Palace** ❻ (Christian VIII's Palæ), originally called the Levetzau Palace. Part of the palace is open all year as a **museum** to the Glücksberg dynasty (tel: 33 12 21 86; www.amalienborgmuseet. dk; May–Oct daily 10am–4pm, Nov–Apr Tue–Sun 11am–4pm; guided tours of the Bel-étage Sat only; charge) – the entrance is by Frederiksgade. Here, you can see the chintzy drawing room of Queen Louise and the studies of Frederik VIII, Frederik IX, Christian IX, and Christian X, which have all been moved from other parts of Amalienborg.

On your right is **Frederik VIII's Palace** ❼ (Frederik VIII's Palæ), with a clock on its facade, which is the home of Crown Prince Frederik and his Australian wife, the Crown Princess Mary Donaldson.

In the centre of the square is an equestrian statue of **Frederik V**, dressed as a Roman emperor. Sculptor Jacques Saly took over 20 years to complete the statue owing, allegedly, to his commitment to having fun. The final price tag was said to have been higher than the cost of the palace itself. The statue here is a copy: the original, unveiled in 1771

Christian IX

Christian IX (1863–1906), for whom one of the Amalienborg palaces is named, came to be known as the 'father-in-law of Europe' because his six children married into the royal families of Sweden, Britain, Russia, Germany and France. A nephew of the childless Frederik VII (1848–63), he was the first king since Christian I (1448–81) not to succeed his father or grandfather, and, although a choice favoured by the Danes, he was not the nearest legal heir. Christian improved his claim by marrying Louise of Hesse, who was more closely related on the female side. His daughter Alexandra married King Edward VII of Britain, son of Queen Victoria.

Gefionspringvandet

with a 21-gun salute, is in the Lapidarium on Slotsholmen (see page 83).

The Marble Church

If you stand with your back to the equestrian statue, you will see the spectacular **Marble Church** ❽ (Marmorkirken; Frederiksgade 4; www.marmorkirken. dk; Mon, Tue, Thu, Sat 10am–5pm; Wed 10am–6.30pm; Fri–Sun noon–5pm; free) or, more properly, 'Frederikskirke'. It was designed as a very important part of the Frederiksstad by Nicolai Eigtved in 1740; yet, 30 years on, it remained unfinished and funds had run out. It languished in ruins for over a century when help came in the guise of an industrialist, Carl Frederik Tietgen, and it was inaugurated in August 1894. A massive dome stands on 12 pillars and is covered in paintings of the 12 apostles, light flooding in from 12 skylights. At 31 metres (101ft) in diameter, the **dome** is second only in size to that of St Peter's in Rome, which measures 42 metres (137ft). You can go up at 1pm and 3pm (daily mid-June–Aug, Sat–Sun rest of year; charge) for some wonderful views.

Outside, at ground level, there are 14 Danish 'Fathers of the Church' and higher up, 18 figures of prophets, apostles and figures from Church history, finishing with Martin Luther.

Alexander Nevsky Church

Coming out of the church, look to your left up Bredgade (an exclusive street full of antique shops and auction houses): you will see the golden onion domes of **Alexander Nevsky Church** ❾ (Alexandr Nevsky Kirke; Bredgade 53; tel: 26 83 51 22 for group visits; Wed 11.30am– 1.30pm), a Russian orthodox church, built in 1883 as a gift from Tsar Alexander III to mark his marriage to Princess Marie Dagmar.

Walk back to Amalienborg and through the square to the waterside, where you will find **Amalie Haven** ❿, a pretty park directly across from the **Opera House** (see page 88).

ALONG THE HARBOUR

Walk along the harbourside, chimneys and windmills visible in the distance, until you reach a copy of Michelangelo's statue of *David*. This heralds the **Royal Cast Collection** ⓫ (Den Kongelige Afstøbningssamling; Vestindisk Pakhus, Toldbodgade 40; tel: 33 74 84 84 10am–2pm; www.smk.dk; Tue 10am– 4pm, Sun 2pm–5pm; free). Set in an 18th-century warehouse, there are copies of over 2,000 famous statues charting the history of sculpture from Ancient Egypt and antiquity onwards.

Walk for another 250 metres/yds along the harbourside until you see the green-topped pavilions on the quayside. It is from here that the royal family take a tender when boarding their yacht *Dannebrog*. Turn left onto **Esplanaden**, which used to be a busy thoroughfare between the docks and **Nyboder**, Christian IV's naval housing estate built in 1631. Turning

Marble Church dome   *Alexandr Nevsky Church*

right along Churchillparken, the fenced-off area on your immediate left was the site of the **Frihedsmuseet** (Resistance Museum), dedicated to exploring the German Occupation in 1940–45. The museum suffered a terrible fire in 2013, and the building was torn down. There are plans to build a new museum here from scratch, for completion in 2018.

Further along Churchillparken are the 19th-century mock-gothic English **Church of St Albans** and the fountain **Gefionspringvandet** (inaugurated in 1909). Commissioned by Carl Jacobsen, the dramatic **statue** ⑫ above the tiers of water shows the goddess Gefion driving a plough and four oxen at great speed. She had tricked the Swedish king, who did not know her identity, into letting her have as much land as she could plough in one night, so she transformed her four giant sons and ploughed enough land to create the island of Sjælland (Zealand).

TOWARDS THE LITTLE MERMAID

Now cross over the bridge behind the *Gefion* fountain back to the waterside. Along the quayside are various statues. The first on your left is of Frederik IX (1947–72), Queen Margrethe's father; a little further on is a bronze bust of one Princess Marie, who died young, hence the mourning mother and child at the base of the statue. Just before you reach *The Little Mermaid*, you will see a tall pillar, topped by a winged Victory, with cannons and canonballs at its base. This is

Huitfeldt Søjlen (The Huitfeldt Column), which commemorates Ivar Huitfeldt, a naval captain who died saving many ships in the battle of Køge Bay against the Swedes in 1710.

Continue on and you will most likely come to a group of tourists; behind them you will find *__The Little Mermaid__* ⑬ (Lille Havfrue, 1913), commissioned by the Carlsberg Foundation in 1909. Edvard Eriksen's small, gentle figure staring out to sea was modelled on his wife Eline. The poor creature has suffered many indignities in her time, including hav-

Marie Dagmar

Marie Dagmar, the second daughter of Christian IX, married the future Tsar Alexander III in St Petersburg in 1866. She had, in fact, been betrothed to Alexander's brother Nicholas in 1864 but he had died suddenly of tuberculous meningitis a few months after their engagement. She became known as Maria Feodorovna and had four sons and two daughters including Tsar Nicholas II and the Grand Duke Michael who were both murdered during the Russian Revolution in 1918. She escaped to London in 1919 and eventually returned to Denmark where she died in 1928. Her funeral was held at Alexander Nevsky Church and she was buried in Roskilde Cathedral where she remained until 2005, when her remains were returned to St Petersburg, as she had wished, to be buried next to her husband.

The church in Kastellet

ing her head chopped off – twice. Now, controversial artist Bjørn Nørgaard has produced *The Genetically Modified Little Mermaid* (2008), a grotesque sculpture that poses on a similar rock 400 metres (1,312ft) from the long-suffering original.

Just beyond the classic mermaid is another Carlsberg commission, *Efter Badet* (After the Bath). Another winged woman (based on an ancient statue of Nike from Samothrace) looks out over the marina from the *Søfartsmonumentet*, created in 1928 in memory of Danish merchant ships and sailors who perished at sea. If you are peckish, walk a little further to **MS Amerika**, see ❸, a popular lunch spot for ferry passengers and local business people.

Kastellet and Nyboder

Follow Langelinie round, cross the bridge, with the marina on your right, and go down the steps to **Kastellet** ⓮, Copenhagen's star-shaped fort, dating from 1662. Over 350 years later, it is still being used by the military. Nonetheless, it is a delightfully peaceful enclave, with 17th- and 18th-century buildings including a church, prison, the commander's house and a gatehouse. There's a charming **windmill** and the grassy ramparts (daily 6am–10pm) are pleasant to walk around.

Walk through Kastellet and you will come back on to Esplanaden. Just opposite stop for a well-earned coffee at **Kafferiet**, see ❹, a small coffee shop in a pale-blue, 18th-century town house. If you are looking for something a bit more

substantial, turn left up Esplanaden towards the harbour until you reach **Lumskebugten**, see ❺.

If you want to have a look at **Nyboder** ⓯, carry on down Esplanaden, away from the harbour, until you reach the grid of ochre-coloured houses. The area's distinctive homes were built by Christian IV in response to a desperate housing shortage for navy personnel. Its inhabitants received free housing and education, but in return all boys went to sea for 16–20 years of compulsory service. Naval law applied to the women and children as well as the men. The single-storeyed houses date back to 1631; the two-storeyed date from the 18th century and the grey-brick buildings are from the 19th century.

Otherwise take the first left down Bredgade, where you will find **Café Petersborg**, see ❻, on your left; or take the second left onto Store Kongensgade for a Copenhagen institution, **Restaurant Ida Davidsen**, see ❼. Further along Bredgade there are two fascinating museums.

Designmuseum Danmark

Set in Frederiksstad's former hospital (1754–1910), the **Designmuseum Danmark** ⓰ (Bredgade 68; www.design museum.dk; Tue–Sun 11am–5pm, Wed until 9pm; charge, under-26s free) is an interesting journey through the history of household design. From Harley Davidsons to cardboard chairs and oriental medieval handicrafts to rococo furniture. Most of the information is in Danish but you can appreciate what you see without too

Designmuseum Danmark   *Ochre-coloured houses in Nyboder*

much information. It also has a pretty garden and an indoor café with good cakes.

The Medical Museum
The **Medical Museum** ⓱ (Medicinsk Museion; Bredgade 62; www.museion.ku.dk; Wed–Fri and Sun noon–4pm; guided tours in English Wed–Fri 2pm, Sun 1.30pm; charge) is next door. Not for the squeamish, but a fascinating collection for anyone interested in the peculiarities and horrors of medicine in a bygone age.

To end on an indulgent note, walk back down to Kongens Nytorv and pop into **Alida Marstrand**, see ⓼, one of Copenhagen's superior chocolatiers.

Food and Drink

❶ RESTAURANT AMALIE
Amaliegade 11; tel: 33 12 88 10; Mon–Sat 11.30am–4pm; €€
This excellent wood-panelled, candlelit lunch restaurant serves up delicious Danish *smørrebrød*. Good value for the quality.

❷ CAFE TOLDBODEN
Amaliegade 41; tel: 33 12 94 67; Mon–Fri 11am–3pm; €€€
Join the local suits who stop for their lunchtime *smørrebrød* in this 18th-century town house. Book to be sure of a seat.

❸ MS AMERIKA
Dampfærgevej 8; tel: 35 26 90 30; Mon–Fri 11am–4pm, Sat–Sun 10am–3pm; €€€
Stop on the west basin for a light lunch of soup, *smørrebrød* or fishcakes.

❹ KAFFERIET
Esplanaden 44; tel:33 93 93 04; Mon–Fri 7.30am–6pm, Sat–Sun 10am–6pm; €
Enjoy excellent double-roast coffee in this quirky café in a duck-egg-blue townhouse.

❺ LUMSKEBUGTEN
Esplanaden 21; tel: 33 15 60 29; Mon–Sat 11.30am–3pm, Wed–Sat 5.30–10pm; €€
Charming, airy restaurant in a former sailors' tavern given to leisurely meals. You may bump into royalty.

❻ CAFE PETERSBORG
Bredgade 76; tel: 33 12 50 16; daily 11.45am–4pm Mon-Sat 6–9pm; €–€€
Excellent Danish café-restaurant in the beamed basement of a house dating from 1746. Go for a *smørrebrød* or a full meal.

❼ RESTAURANT IDA DAVIDSEN
Store Kongensgade 70; tel: 33 91 36 55; Mon–Fri 10.30am–4pm; €€
This pricey *smørrebrød* restaurant is a Copenhagen institution dating from 1888, with a choice of 250 sandwiches.

❽ ALIDA MARSTRAND
Bredgade 14; Tue–Fri 11am–5pm, Sat 10am–1pm, €€
This small chocolatier opened in 1930, with confectionary recipes gleaned from the Tzar's court, including traditional marzipan pigs.

Ornately tiled stove in the David Collection

AROUND ROSENBORG

Rosenborg Slot seems remarkable not just for its beauty but also its position bang in the middle of Copenhagen, surrounded by elegant town houses, the botanical gardens and a couple of lovely art galleries.

DISTANCE: 2km (1.5 miles)
TIME: A half/full day
START: David Collection
END: Hirschsprung Collection
POINTS TO NOTE: If you find yourself short on time, visit Rosenborg Palace and the National Gallery of Art (see page 60) and just walk through the King's Gardens and the botanical gardens. The latter make for a welcoming break if you have had your dose of historical artefacts and paintings.

The Dutch Renaissance-style castle Rosenborg is a real highlight of the city. However, when the architect-king Christian IV built it in 1606, it actually stood outside Copenhagen, in the country-side beyond the north-eastern ramparts. Christiansborg was a crumbling mess at the time, and the royal residence of Frederiksborg lay an inconvenient 35km (22 miles) away, so it made sense to have a palace closer to the city.

Rosenborg was built in several stages (see page 56); by 1624, it was much

as it is today. It is still surrounded by the pretty **King's Gardens** (Kongens Have), a welcome green area, and extremely popular with Copenhageners. Around three million people come to stroll, sunbathe and picnic here each year. The Parkmuseerne combined ticket (http://parkmuseerne.dk) offers a discount on entry to the castle, the Filmhouse (Filmhuset) and three museums: the Hirschsprung Collection, the National Gallery of Art and the Natural History Museum.

The most impressive way to approach Rosenborg is through the gardens from the Kronprinsessegade gate. However, before you go in, take half an hour or so in the **David Collection ❶** (Davids Samling; Kronprinsessegade 30–32; www.davidmus.dk; Tue–Sun 10am–5pm, Wed until 9pm), a lovely collection of European fine arts and Islamic and far-eastern art from the 7th to the 19th centuries.

The collection is housed in an old town house – worth a visit in itself – on a street that, until the fire of 1795, was part of the King's Gardens. After the fire, King Frederik VI donated a strip of land to the

The King's Gardens in winter

city and a long line of neoclassical houses was built. The sale of these financed rebuilding in the Old Town. At the same time, 12 little shop-pavilions were built along the park's edge. The buildings, with a floor space of 16 sq metres (53 sq ft), are still in use today.

KING'S GARDENS

From the entrance to the **King's Gardens** ❷ (Kongens Have; daily from 7am, closing times vary from Jan 5pm to July 11pm; free), you will see the best view of the turreted romantic castle, straight down the crocus lawn (finest in spring), lined with marble spheres dating from 1674. The castle sits on its own island within the gardens, and is accessed by the Grønnebro (Green Bridge) over the moat.

The gardens originally provided the palace with fish from three fish ponds and fruit and vegetables from orchards and vegetable gardens. Even when the castle became state property in 1849, Rosenborg continued to furnish the royal family with fresh produce until 1909. Wander at will or follow the route below to see the gardens' main attractions before visiting the castle.

Krumspringet

Turn left at the Kronprinsessegade entrance and walk around the edge of the park until you come to the third path on your right. Turn right and right again to visit the **Krumspringet ❹**, a maze of narrow paths arranged in a symmetrical pattern. This one is modern, but old garden plans show that there was a maze in the gardens back in the 17th century. The name comes from the Danish for 'dodge' as people could avoid unwanted meetings by nipping out of the way down one of its many paths. Walk to the

The armory at Rosenborg Castle

centre and then out again, by the next path on the right, which will bring you to the **crocus lawn ⑧**, which is truly spectacular in spring.

Hans Christian Andersen

With the castle on your left, continue down the Allé. For a civilised coffee break, branch off diagonally for the **Orangeriet**, see ①, or head straight on to the **Hans Christian Andersen statue ⓒ**. Sculptor August Saaybe had envisaged children listening to the storyteller, but Andersen objected, saying that he hated having anyone sitting close to him when he read and that his fairytales were intended as much for adults as children. The statue was eventually unveiled in 1880, after his death. There are some attractive reliefs depicting his stories around the plinth.

Palace Architecture

First built in 1606 by Christian IV as a summer residence, the palace consisted of the core of the south side of the palace that we know today; two storeys high with a spire-crowned turret facing the city and two bays to the east. In 1611, the central gate tower and drawbridge were added. Further work was done in 1613–15, with an additional two-story wing built on the north side of the gate tower; then another floor (containing the Knights' Hall) was added across the whole building in 1616 along with the spire-crowned towers, and completed in 1624.

Hercules Pavilion and Statue

Turn back and take the first right. Head past a playground and then take the next right to see the **Hercules Pavilion ⓓ** and a modern **statue of Hercules and the Lion ⓔ** performing the first of his 12 Labours: strangling the Nemean Lion with his bare hands in an attempt to atone for a moment of madness and the murder of his three children. The original marble, bought by Frederik IV in 1708–9 on a trip to Italy, crumbled away: this is a modern copy.

The pavilion (now a café) first known as the 'Blue Arbour', was altered by Christian V so that his family could eat without the servants being present. Beyond the pavilion is the 20th-century **herbaceous border ⓕ**, which is over 250 metres (820ft) in length and has over 200 plants that change seasonally.

Taking a right and then a left will bring you to the **Rose Garden ⓖ**, which is laid out in a 16th-century design at the side of the palace. The statue at the end is by the famous sculptor Vilhelm Bissen and depicts Caroline Amalie (1796–1881), wife of Christian VIII, who became queen in 1839. The royal pair were happily married but did not have any children.

Now cross the castle moat, guarded by two green copper lions. One of the original 17th-century beasts was smashed apart in 1744 by three soldiers, to get at the silver coins that passersby had tossed in through a crack – they were flogged, branded and sentenced to a life in slavery for their crime.

The King's Gardens   *Royal regalia in Rosenborg Castle*

ROSENBORG CASTLE

Rosenborg Castle ❸ (Rosenborg Slot; Øster Volgade 4A; www.rosenborgslot.dk; June–Aug daily 10am–5pm, May, Sept and Oct daily 10am–4pm, Jan–Apr and Nov–Dec Tue–Sun 10am–2pm; charge) is an absolute must-see, bursting with rich detail and unusual objects (such as a joke chair from the 17th century, which squirted its victims with water). However, it is worth buying a guidebook, as there is very little English information inside.

The interior of the castle charts (chronologically) the tastes and needs of different kings from Christian IV in the 17th century to Frederik IV, his great-grandson, in the 18th. It was the monarch's primary residence until 1710, when Frederik IV moved out. Since then, it has been used briefly as a residence on two occasions; in 1794 after the fire at Christiansborg and in 1801, when the British bombarded Copenhagen.

On the ground floor, the private **royal apartments** contain the bedroom in which Christian IV died in 1648 (having been carried from Frederiksborg expressly for the purpose) and a fully tiled, blue-and-white Delft toilet with an embossed ceiling, and the **State Apartments**, including the **Knights' Hall** on the second floor, are packed with solid-silver furniture and countless artefacts alluding to Denmark's success on the world stage.

In the basement, behind massive doors guarded by soldiers, are the Crown Jewels and other exotic royal regalia. The jewels were originally bequeathed for the use of the reigning queen by Queen Sophie Magdalene, 'because', she wrote in her will in 1746, 'in this Royal Family there have been so few jewels, and no Crown Jewels at all'. The Treasury includes other exotic items, such as swords, crowns, a legendary hunting horn, and silver boxes containing the umbilical cords of Frederik III's children.

Before you leave, visit the **Pleasure Garden** on the south side of the palace. It's based on the 17th-century original, in

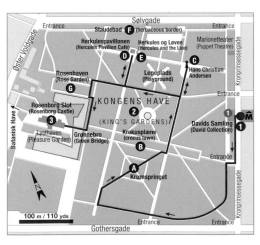

Bird of Paradise flower

which exotic plants were planted to stand alone for dramatic impact. Exit onto Øster Voldgade at the back of the castle, and turn left. Either cross the road for the entrance to the **Botanical Gardens** or take a short detour down to Gothersgade to visit the **Workers' Museum**.

THE WORKERS' MUSEUM

For the **Workers' Museum ❹** (Arbejdermuseet; Rømersgade 22; www.arbejdermuseet.dk; daily 10am–4pm; charge) ond left on to Rømersgade, where you

The Golden Age

The Danish Golden Age spanned the first half of the 19th century and was a time of new ideas and great creativity in the arts. The leading proponents all lived in Copenhagen, then a small city of 10,000 inhabitants, and would have known each other and exchanged ideas. Ironically, as art and culture flourished, Denmark was suffering economically and politically. Important cultural figures at this time were the artist Christoffer Eckersberg who introduced a new naturalism and intimacy to painting; C.F. Hansen, the inspired classical architect, who was responsible for rebuilding many of Copenhagen's buildings after the 1795 fire; the great fairytale writer Hans Christian Andersen; the philosopher Søren Kirkegaard; the ballet choreographer August Bournonville; and the sculptor Bertel Thorvaldsen.

will find the museum a short way down on the left.

Housed in the former Danish Workers' Movement building, the museum is dedicated to the history of the worker in Denmark. Permanent displays focus on daily life, using models and mannequins to tell each story: a two-room flat belonging to the Sørensen family dates from before World War I; a 1930s flat is home to the impoverished, out-of-work Petersen family; the prosperity of the 1950s is seen through the recreation of a coffee shop, shopping street and typical working family's flat; and there's an exhibition on industrial work conditions. The workers' original beer hall is now **Café & Ølhalle 1892**, see ❷.

BOTANICAL GARDENS

Return to walk through the **Botanical Gardens ❺** (Botanisk Have; Øster Farimagsgade 2B; daily May–Sept 8.30am–6pm, Oct–Mar 8.30am–4pm; free), another lovely green space in the city.

The present gardens, dating from 1872, are in fact the city's fourth; the first botanical gardens in Copenhagen were founded in 1600. Altogether they cover 10 hectares (25 acres) and are home to around 9,000 different plant species. There are lakes and ponds, pretty bridges, plenty of benches with attractive views and a restored **Palm House**, based on the one at Kew Gardens in Surrey, England. The gardens form part of the National History

The lily-pond   *Golden Barrel Cactus*

Museum, along with two small museums found in the grounds, the **Botanical Museum** (Botanisk Museum; open for exhibitions) and the **Geology Museum** (Geologisk Museum; Øster Voldgade 5–7; http://geologi.snm. ku.dk; Tue–Sun 10–4pm; charge).

Repair to the café before heading to your next port of call, the **Hirschsprung Collection**, situated in the grounds of the National Gallery of Art (see page 60).

HIRSCHSPRUNG COLLECTION

Exit the gardens onto Sølvgade. Turn right for the National Gallery of Art; otherwise, turn left and then right up Stockholmsgade for the **Hirschsprung Collection ❻** (Hirschsprungske Samling; Stockholmsgade 20; www.hirschsprung. dk; daily 11am–4pm; charge, free Wed). This charming 100-year-old art gallery (housed in a neoclassical villa designed especially for the collection) stands in the grassy grounds of the Østre Anlæg park, on the site of the old city ramparts.

The paintings and sculptures, which make up an important collection of Danish art from the period known as the 'Golden Age' (1800–50), were gifted to the nation by tobacco tycoon Heinrich Hirschsprung (1836–1908). It is an intimate museum with the art displayed as it might be in a private residence, surrounded by period furniture and artefacts from the artists' homes and studios. Artists featured include those from the Skagen group, the Symbolists and C.W.

Eckersberg, who is credited with laying the foundations for the Golden Age.

For lunch, you could try the good, but rather pricey, café in the National Gallery of Art or, better still, make your way to **Aamanns**, see ❸.

Food and Drink

❶ ORANGERIET

Kongens Have/Kronprinsessegade 13; tel: 33 11 13 07; Mon–Sat 11.30am– midnight, kitchen closes at 10pm, Sun noon–4pm; €€€

This top-quality pavilion restaurant has views from every window of the King's Garden. Perfect for a glass of wine and immaculate *smørrebrød* on the sunny terrace, or return for a romantic evening meal.

❷ CAFE & ØLHALLE 1892

Rømersgade 22; tel: 31 15 34 55; Mon– Sat 11am–5pm; €

A good selection of Danish food and beer, including 'Stjerne (Star) Pilsner' that still bears the original 1947 label.

❸ AAMANNS

10–12 Øster Farimagsgade; tel: 35 55 33 44; deli: Mon–Sun noon–4pm, last order 2.30pm, Wed–Sat 6–11pm, kitchen closes 9.30pm; €–€€€

Fabulous deli offering *smørrebrød* masterpieces. The next-door bistro upholds the quality, with its innovative New Nordic dishes.

The original building dates back to 1896

THE NATIONAL GALLERY OF ART

The Statens Museum for Kunst is Denmark's national art gallery. Housed in a building that reflects two centuries of design, its world-class collection spans 700 years of national and international art.

> **DISTANCE:** n/a – the whole tour is spent within the museum
> **TIME:** A half/full day
> **START:** Level 1: Sculpture Street
> **END:** Level 2: Rooms 260–272
> **POINTS TO NOTE:** This visit can be as short or as long as you like to make it. At a fairly brisk pace, you can cover most of it in about two hours, but you will enjoy it more if you give it a bit more time.

You cannot fail to be impressed by Denmark's **National Gallery of Art** (Statens Museum for Kunst; Sølvgade 48–50; www.smk.dk; Tue, Thu–Sun 10am–5pm, Wed 10am–8pm; permanent collection free, charge for exhibitions). The original collection, once the private collection of the king, first went on show to the public in 1822 at Christiansborg Palace. Fortunately, it escaped the palace fire in 1884 and the National Gallery of Art, designed by Vilhelm Dahlerup, was opened in 1886. Today, its high,

airy foyer, winding staircase and view through to the collections beyond are the result of an impressive redesign and the removal of a large central staircase in the 1960s. The collection underwent a dramatic three-year rehang recently, to reflect a more contemporary view of art history.

Children are very welcome at the museum; ring ahead or ask at the reception desk about activities on offer. Prams and push-chairs must be left outside, but locks and waterproof covers are available from reception. There are free push-chairs available for use in the entrance hall. Lockers are also available for bags larger than A4 size.

LEVEL 1

As you walk into the entrance hall, the temporary exhibition spaces are to the left and right. At the time of writing, forthcoming exhibitions included: *Portrayers of Humanity*, a study of fear and anxiety post-WWII (September 2015 to January 2016); and *Eckers-*

Sculpture in the museum gardens

berg (October 2015 to January 2016), an in-depth look at the 19th-century Father of Danish painting.

To get your bearings and to explore the interesting mix of old and new architecture in the various gallery buildings, walk through the entrance hall, down the steps to **Sculpture Street ❶**, which runs across the back of the old 19th-century building in a striking glass-roofed extension. Here you'll find the latest sculpture exhibitions and large-scale installations (past exhibitions works have included, for example, Danish artist FOS's warped buildings, glowing yellow tents and curious machines).

Directly ahead is a set of wide steps, actually the seats of an **amphitheatre ❷**. At the back of its stage is a glass wall, through which you can see the water and greenery of Øster Anlæg, the park at the back of the museum. To the left is a small **children's workshop area ❸** (Sat–Sun 10.30am–4.30pm; charge), where professional artists help kids to explore their creativity; enter via the stairs on Sculpture Street. Nearby is the **x-rummet ❹**, containing works commissioned by contemporary artists especially for this unusual space.

LEVEL 2

The second level is home to the collections. Take the lift in the main entrance hall to Level 2, to the landing opposite Room 201.

European Art 1300–1800

Room 201A contains an overview of the gallery's impressive collection of European art ❺, which includes works by Titian, El Greco and Rubens. Particularly intriguing in this room is Lucas Cranach the Elder's oil-on-wood *Melancholy* (1532), an allegorical work in which an angel apparently rues man's predilection for violence.

Three routes wend their way chronologically through the European section, tracing artists from Italy, the Netherlands and Northern Europe.

Route 1, focusing on Italian art, begins around the corner in **Room 201B** with examples of Renaissance and Gothic art, including the glowering marble sculpture *Head of a Bearded Man* (1312) by Giovanni Pisano and the lovely *Meeting of St Anne and St Joachim at the Golden Gate* by Filipino Lippi (1497). There are also two handsome El Greco portraits and a Titian. Seventeenth-century artworks include Salvator Rosa's emotionally-charged *Diogenes Throwing Away his Drinking Cup* (1651), black with stormclouds.

In **Room 201E** internal torment gives way to an 18th-century interest in Italian travel and land- and cityscapes, with some beautiful paintings by Tiepolo and Guardi.

Route 2, looking at art from the Netherlands, threads through a suite of small rooms (211B to 209) holding works by Thomas de Keyser, Wil-

Melancholy, by Lucas Cranach the Elder

lem Kolf, Balthasar van der Ast and Adrien de Vries, a Dutch Mannerist sculptor. **Room 209** contains an interesting collection of works from Rembrandt's workshop.

Route 3 covers the rest of Northern Europe. It begins with a question – what does it mean to be a 'good man'? – and answers it in **Rooms 202 and 203** with works including an altar panel by Petrus Christus dating from 1450; Cranach's

famous *Portrait of Martin Luther* (the two were friends), dating from the height of the Reformation; the comic but faintly unsettling *Strife of Lent with Shrovetide* by Bruegel the Elder; and Cornelis de Vos's *Judgement Day*.

Room 204 is dedicated to Rubens (1577–1640), with portraits of *Francesco de' Medici* and *Joanna of Austria*, and Rubens' masterpiece, *The Judgement of Solomon* (1617).

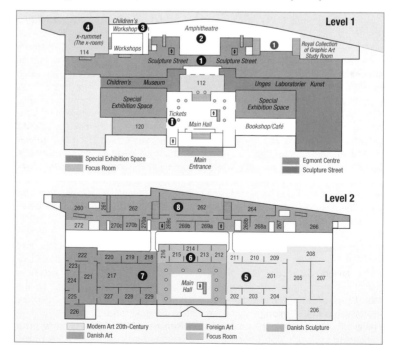

Still Life with Door, Guitar and Bottles, by Pablo Picasso

Cross Room 205, and enter **Room 206**, containing examples of painstaking and detailed *trompe l'oeil*. **Rooms 207** and **208A** nod to the Danes' 17th- and 18th-century love of all things French, with work by Nattier and Fragonard amongst others, and lead you round again to **Room 205**, where you can check out the delicacy of the butterfly placement in Cornelisz van Haarlem's *Fall of the Titans* (1599–90), alongside other Northern European History Paintings.

French Art 1900–30

Retrace your steps to the landing above the foyer, where **Rooms 212–216** ❻ contain a real treat: pieces by international artists who were part of the early 20th-century Parisian art scene. Highlights include several works by Matisse (1869–1954) in **Room 214**, including the famous *Portrait of Madame Matisse* (1905), also known as *The Green Line*, which gave rise to the name of the French splinter art group, The Fauves (or 'wild animals'), whose work was characterised by a strong use of intuitive colour. The Matisses were gathered by a far-sighted engineer, Johannes Rump, who donated them in 1928.

The gallery also owns 68 works, mainly etchings and lithographs, by Pablo Picasso: two still lives in oil are on display in **Room 213**, along with a prize Modigliani, *Alice* (1918). The *embarras de richesses* doesn't stop there: other great artists on display include Dufy (**Room 212**); Braque and Gris (**Room 213**); Derain (**Room 215**); and Léger (**Room 216**).

Danish and Nordic Art 1750–1900

Back on the landing, turn right into **Rooms 217–29** ❼, a section dedicated to Danish and Nordic art that includes the period 1800–50, an era known as the Golden Age (see page 58) in which the arts flourished, new ideas and styles came to the fore, and, in the arts, a turning to nature and the everyday condition of the world and its inhabitants was paramount. **Room 217**, divided into six sections, gives an overview, which continues in **Rooms 218–20** (turn right as you leave 217F). C.W. Eckersberg, a Golden-Age giant, is well represented with *Bella and Hanna* (1820); *A View through Three of the Colosseum's North-Western Arches* (1815); and *Russian Ship of the Line 'Asow'* (1828).

Other rooms in this section are themed. **Room 221** – 'The Body in Art' – includes *Evening Talk* (1889), a study in strained body language, by the angst-ridden Edvard Munch; and Ejnar Nielsen's raw and mesmerising *And in his Eyes I saw Death* (1897), in which a hollow-eyed figure looking like a young Omar Sharif waits by a coffin, staring blankly ahead.

Rooms 223–224 explore the emergence of modern-day Denmark:

J.F. Willumsen's A Mountain Climber (detail; 1912)

highlights include Anna Ancher's *A Funeral* (1891); Michael Ancher's *The Lifeboat is Taken Through the Dunes* (1883); and works by P.S. Krøyer, including the light-filled, dreamlike *Boys Bathing at Skagen. Summer Evening* (1899); all of whom were strongly influenced by French Impressionism.

Room 228 is dedicated to Vilhelm Hammershøi's trademark grey works (washed-out interiors, muted portraits and ghostly paintings of Copenhagen's buildings), and features *Portrait of Ida Ilsted* (1898), recently saved for the nation thanks to a large donation from the charitable foundation

Part of the museum's modern art collection

Augustinus Fonden. Imbued with light and cheer, **Room 229** – 'Willumsen and Vitalism' – contains Johannes Larsen's sun-splashed *Children Playing, Enghave Square* (1908) and J.F. Willumsen's *Mountain Climber* (1912), a statuesque woman in perfect harmony with the landscape.

Danish and International Art from 1900

From the landing, cross a bridge over Sculpture Street to **Rooms 260–272** ❽, which are dedicated to modern art. The long walkway forms a timeline, with the large exhibition rooms overlooking Østre Anlæg park containing a chronological progression of works from 1900 to the present day. The smaller rooms on the other side focus on particular artists or themes, and pieces are rotated more regularly.

The museum's modern collection contains some particularly fine pieces, especially by the CoBrA group, a collective of post-war avant-garde artists from Copenhagen, Brussels and Amsterdam. Their colourful works tended towards the surreal, with an abstract distortion of images often borrowed from primitive and folk art. Carl-Henning Pedersen, known as the 'Scandinavian Chagall', was a founder member: his paintings are filled with cosmic imagery, dominated by abstract, otherworldly birds. Just before his death in 2007, Pedersen donated 40 works to the gallery.

The gallery's airy interior

Among his most famous are *People and Animals in a Landscape* (1942), *The Turkish Drum* (1960) and *Out Into the Wide World* (1988), not on display at the time of writing.

Even better known is fellow CoBrA founder Asger Jorn, a political radical and prolific artist who produced some 2,500 paintings, sculptures, prints and tapestries during his lifetime, as well as fomenting rebellion against the 'established' art world. Works include *Red Visions* (1944) and his almost fairytale-like *Wheel of Life* (1953), a universal and timeless theme that he took up after recovering from tuberculosis in 1951, currently on display in **Room 269B**.

Bjørn Nørgaard (b.1947), a prominent member of the current Danish art scene, is well represented in the gallery's collection. Daring and challenging works include the iconic photo series *The Female Christ* (1969) and the 17-minute film *Horse Sacrifice* (1970), which both caused a huge furore in their day: objects recovered from the latter can be seen in **Room 263B**. Over time, Nørgaard has become a royal favourite, designing 11 tapestries for Christiansborg Palace as well as Queen Margrethe's sarcophagus.

The gallery also holds almost 300 pieces by another of Denmark's greats, Per Kirkeby (b.1938), who has spent more than four decades exploring broad metaphysical concepts.

Landscape and nature are recurring themes, depicted with characteristically vigorous, thickly-textured brushstrokes. In commenting on his thought processes as he paints, Kirkeby rather comfortingly says that if he makes a mistake, 'it doesn't matter much; I can always paint over it'.

There are several installations of the love-'em-or-hate-'em kind, such as subversive creations by Danish/Norwegian collaborators Michael Elmgreen and Ingar Dragset in **Room 302C**: as the door swings shut behind you, *Please, Keep Quiet!* (2003) unnerves visitors with its detailed reconstruction of a hospital ward.

To take a break and digest all the artwork that you have seen, head to the café on Level 1, see ❶. The bookshop, on the same floor, has an excellent range of art books and National Gallery publications.

Food and Drink

❶ CAFÉEN

Level 1, Staten Museum for Kunst; tel: 33 74 84 94; Tue–Sun 10am–4.50pm, Wed 10am–7.50pm, last orders 30 minutes before closing; €€
Lovely fresh food, all cooked on the spot and served in stylish surroundings. The café was designed by artists Bjørn Nørgaard and Peter Lassen and offers great views across Østre Anlæg park.

Dronning Louises Bro

NØRREBRO AND ALONG THE RESERVOIRS

The main things to do in Nørrebro are walking in the cemetery on a nice day and meandering around the shopping streets around Sankt Hans Torv. Weather permitting, the reservoirs are a pleasant spot for a walk or jog.

> **DISTANCE:** 4km (3 miles)
> **TIME:** A half day
> **START:** Drønnings Louise Bro
> **END:** Tycho Brahe Planetarium
> **POINTS TO NOTE:** It's a long walk from the centre: bus 5A from Rådhuspladsen to Dronning Louises Brø will shorten the journey.

Nørrebro (North Bridge) lies beyond the reservoirs. It started off as a staunch working-class district in the 19th century. It still has a reputation for political activism, and is a lively, multicultural place to hang out or shop.

Start on the city side of **Dronning Louises Bro ❶** (Bridge), a popular gathering point for public demonstrations. On your left is **Peblinge Sø** (lake), while on your right is **Sortedams Sø**.

Walk down Nørrebrogade and turn left on Blågardsgade passing through **Blågards Plads ❷**. This avenue once lead to Blågård mansion, named for its distinctive blue roof tiles, which burnt down in 1835. On your left, note the 22 granite statues along the edges of the sunken square (where a few beer drinkers may be hanging out). They were carved on site by sculptor Kai Nielsen who used the locals as his inspiration. Cross the square and turn right up Korsgade as far as Kapelvej. Turn right at Helligkors Kirke, following the street around until you reach the entrance to the cemetery on your left.

ASSISTENS KIRKEGAARD

This **churchyard ❸** (daily Apr–Sept 7am–10pm, Oct–Mar 7am–7pm; free) is very popular with the locals, especially in summer, when you will see plenty of joggers, sunbathers and mothers with buggies. It was laid out in 1760 to relieve pressure on the city graveyards, which were full to overflowing after several outbreaks of plague had killed over one third of the population (23,000 people) in just 50 years. The main entrance is

Laundry and lattes at the Laundromat Café

between two urn-topped red-brick gate posts. For the grave of Hans Christian Andersen (see page 56), take the lefthand pathway inside the entrance. Follow the righthand path to see a map of famous graves, including H.C. Andersen, Søren Kierkegaard, Niels Bohr and Dan Turréll; a little beyond, the red-brick building Kulturcentret Assistens has paper maps.

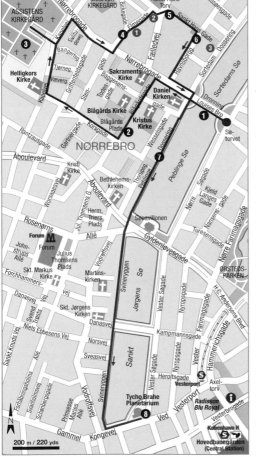

Come out of the same gate, walk left along Kappelvej, then turn right onto Nørrebrogade. Cross the road and walk down to **Elmegade ❹**, a popular shopping street. Browse in the likes of Foxy Lady, Fünf and Radical Zoo for streetwise clothing and accessories. For a coffee or a bite to eat, drop into the **Laundromat Café**, see ❶, or keep on until you reach **Sankt Hans Torv ❺**, the central place to hang out in summer. There are several cafés with outdoor seating; connoisseurs could also try coffee-bean specialists **Kaffeplantagen**, see ❷.

Cross the square and walk down Sankt Hans

Café life on Sankt Hans Torv

Gade. At the first junction, you can either continue on to **Café 22**, see ❸. or turn right on to **Ravnsborggade** ❻, which is full of bric-a-brac and antique shops. At the end, turn left onto Nørrebrogade. Just before Dronning Louises Bro, turn right down **Peblinge Dossering** ❼, stopping to enjoy the view from one of many reservoir-side benches.

Continue alongside the water to the **Tycho Brahe Planetarium** ❽ (Gammel Kongevej 10; http://planetariet.dk; Mon noon–7.30pm, Tue and Sun 10.30am–7.30pm, Wed–Thu 9.30am–7.30pm, Fri–Sat 10.30am–8.30pm; charge), which has one or two interesting displays and an IMAX cinema.

Food and Drink

❶ LAUNDROMAT CAFÉ

Elmegade 15; tel: 35 35 26 72; Mon–Fri 8am–11pm, Sat–Sun 9am–11pm; €
One of Copenhagen's first 'hybrid' cafés, Laundromat just celebrated its 10th birthday. Do your washing, buy second-hand books, and indulge in an excellent breakfast or brunch.

❷ KAFFEPLANTAGEN

Sankt Hans Torv 3; tel: 32 11 41 14; Mon–Fri 8am–10pm, Sat–Sun 9am–10pm; €
Coffee-bean specialists brew one of the best cups of coffee in Copenhagen. Window seats have big comfy cushions perfect for relaxing.

❸ CAFÉ 22

Sortedam Dossering 21; tel: 35 37 38 27; Sun–Wed 9am–midnight, Thu–Sat 9am–1am; €€
Attractive decor and reasonable food. The real appeal is the outdoor lakeside seating, where you can sit and watch the swans.

Tycho Brahe Planetarium

Leafy Fredericksberg

FREDERIKSBERG

Leafy Frederiksberg is Copenhagen's upmarket – formerly royal – suburb, and home to Frederiksberg Slot, Søndermarken and the underground Cisternerne art space, the zoo and attractive, tree-lined, residential boulevards. Although so close to the centre, it is a municipality independent of Copenhagen.

DISTANCE: 2km (1.25 miles)
TIME: A full day
START: Frederiksberg Runddel
END: Memorial Mound
POINTS TO NOTE: This walk works well in both directions – in summer the zoo is open late, so it makes sense to go there last; in winter you may want to go there first. You can also tack this walk, or part of it, onto the Vesterbro walk (see page 28). Turn right at the top of Ny Carlsberg Vej, cross the road and up some steps into Søndermarken. Follow the path to Frederiksberg Castle and the zoo.

Until the 18th century, Frederiksberg was a small country village. It rose to prominence as the concept of a country retreat began to appeal to middle-class and wealthy town dwellers. These included Frederik IV who, inspired by his travels in Italy, built a summer palace in the grounds of a former royal farm at the end of Frederiksberg Allé.

This walk starts at **Frederiksberg Runddel** ❶, in front of the park gates. Every winter (Nov–Mar), there is an outdoor skating rink here. This is not far from the junction of Vesterbrogade and **Frederiksberg Allé**, formerly the rather grand private road that led to the castle. When you walk along this major boulevard you will pass several theatres, a war memorial and **Frederiksberg Chokolade**, an excellent chocolate shop, see ❶. As you approach the *runddel* (square), you will pass a cemetery on your left belonging to **Frederiksberg Church**. To visit the church, turn left onto Pile Allé.

FREDERIKSBERG CHURCH

Frederiksberg Church ❷ (Frederiksberg Kirke; Frederiksberg Allé 65; daily 8am–5pm), with its pyramidal roof, was built in the Baroque style by architect Felix Dusart in 1732–34 and is notable for its octagonal shape, the first of its kind in Denmark. Inside, there are four attractive, green-painted wooden galleries, which were added in 1864. Many important Danes are buried in the graveyard, including figures from the Danish 'Golden Age'

Grey heron, Fredericksberg Gardens

(see page 58), such as the poet Adam Oehlenschläger and his children.

ALLÉGADE

Before entering the park opposite, turn right and walk up **Allégade** ❸, a pretty street lined with restaurants and cafés set back from the road. This is one of Frederiksberg's oldest streets, dating from the 1650s when the first farmers settled here. Since the end of the 18th century, it has also been the place to have fun and in 1784, there were 34 pubs ranged along here. **Allégade 10**, on your right, dates from this period.

On your left, as you walk up, there is also the **Museum of Danish Revue Theatre** ❹ (Revymuseet; Allégade 5; Tue–Sun 11am–4pm; charge), a cele-bration of Danish music-hall and variety acts that may be lost on non-Danes.

STORM P MUSEUM

Return to Frederiksberg Runddel, where you will find the main entrance to the park. On the left is a delightful small museum, the **Storm P Museum** ❺ (Storm P Museet; Frederiksberg Runddel; tel: 38 86 05 23; Tue–Sun 10am–4pm; charge), which is dedicated to the cartoonist and humourist Robert Storm Petersen.

This witty Danish cartoonist's work seems to combine the social realism of the late 19th and early 20th centuries with the ludicrous inventions of Heath Robinson and some of the cartoon quali-ties of Mr Magoo. You need to understand some Danish to fully appreciate the car-

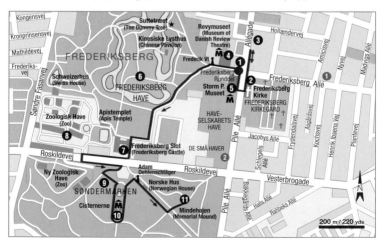

Frederiksberg Castle　　　　　*The bridge to the Chinese Pavilion*

toons, but the museum is still worth a visit to see their visual style and humour.

FREDERIKSBERG GARDENS

If lunch or supper is looming, visit one of the three small, very traditional Danish restaurants called 'De Små Haver' (The Small Gardens), next to the Frederiksberg Gardens (Frederiksberg Have), before you go any further: **Hansens Gamle Familiehave**, see ❷, is open all year-round.

Enter the **park** ❻ through the main gate (daily from 6am; closing times vary from July 11pm to Jan 5pm; free). In the 19th century, there used to be a guard here charged with keeping out anyone he considered undesirable (including seamen and people with dogs).

Just inside the gates there is a **statue of King Frederik VI** (1808–39) by H.W. Bissen. Frederik VI, cousin to Britain's king, George VI, governed as Regent from 1784 and was responsible for abolishing serfdom in 1788. He was also Regent during the British attacks on Copenhagen in 1801 and 1807. The inscription on the plinth translates as, 'Here he felt happy in the midst of loyal people'.

There is a park map at the entrance. To the right, you will find yourself walking (or better still, rowing – boats can be hired from May to September) around the meandering canal system within the park. Turn left and walk along the side of the park for the quickest route to Frederiksberg Castle and the zoo.

The park was originally a formal Baroque garden but in 1798–1804 was remodelled in the fashionable English 'Romantic' style, complete with picturesque follies. These include the **Chinese Pavilion** (May–Aug: Sun 2–4pm; free); the **Møstings House**, a listed, pretty neoclassical house; the **Swiss House**, a little cottage built for the royal family to take tea; and the colonnaded **Apis Temple**. A colony of grey herons nests to the east of the Chinese pavilion. The males arrive in March and the females in May – they can often be seen wandering the lawns and paths. If you walk that way, look out for the Dummy Tree (Suttetræet), on whose branches generations of Danish children have hung their final, out-grown dummy (pacifier).

Frederiksberg Castle ❼ (Frederiksberg Slot; closed to the public), standing at the south end of the gardens, is now a military academy. Walk up to its terrace and admire the view along the broad axis that is part of the original Baroque design. In the 19th century, you could see as far as the Sound from here.

Leave via the exit on the other side of the castle and turn right, walking down Roskildevej until you reach the zoo. The park opposite is **Søndermarken**, and the far end of Vesterbro (see page 28) lies on the other side.

THE ZOO

The **Zoo** ❽ (Roskildevej 32; www.zoo.dk; July 10am–8pm; June–Aug 10am–6pm; Apr, May and Sept–Oct 10am–5pm;

Lions at the zoo

Jan–Mar and Nov–Dec: 10am–4pm; charge) is not just of interest to children, especially on a sunny summer evening. As zoos go, it is an excellent one, with lots on offer, including elephants in an enclosure designed by Norman Foster, tigers, brown bears, polar bears and a marvellous pride of lions. There is a viewing. tower, and a café close to the entrance

SØNDERMARKEN

Opposite the zoo is another garden **Søndermarken** ❾ (daily 24 hours; free). **Cisternerne** is in sight of the road (the entrance is inside one of the two glass pyramids), and the **Memorial Mound** is down a path to your left.

Cisternerne ❿ (Søndermarken; www.cisternerne.dk; Apr–Nov Tue–Sun 11am–5pm; charge) is worth a visit for its location alone. An underground reservoir built to supply the city with water after the cholera epidemic of 1853, its arches stretch out in all directions like a crypt and are hung with spindly limestone stalactites. It's an eerie, atmospheric space, used for changing art exhibitions and intense, immersive electronic music performances – see the website for upcoming events.

Walk back towards the castle and turn right. You will pass a **statue of the poet Adam Oehlenschläger**, who ran around the park as a child because his father was the Palace Steward, and the **Norwegian House**, a romantic folly dating from 1787, before reaching the

mound ⓫ (open 4 July only) on your left. It is surrounded by tall trees and commemorates Denmark's emigrants. The words above the entrance translate, 'They who set out, never to return'. Inside, at the end of a stone passage, there is a cavern, a cupola letting in light above the life-size figure of a woman representing Mother Denmark, who is embracing her children.

The easiest way to get back to the centre of town is on the No. 6A bus from outside the zoo.

Food and Drink

❶ FREDERIKSBERG CHOKOLADE

Frederiksberg Allé 64; Mon–Wed 10am–5.30pm, Thu–Fri 10am–6pm, Sat 10am–3pm; €€
Exquisite handmade cakes and chocolates. Highlights include realistic-looking chocolate flowers – or how about a chocolate chess set? Also runs courses, if you want to learn their secrets.

❷ HANSENS GAMLE FAMILIEHAVE

Pile Allé 16; tel: 36 30 92 57; www.hansenshave.dk; mid-Apr–Sept daily 11am–midnight; Oct–mid-Apr closed Sun eve and Mon, also closed Tue in Jan and Feb; €–€€
This cosy old-fashioned place – with its checked tablecloths, twinkly lights and traditional Danish *smørrebrød* – dates back to 1850, when it sold boiling water to park visitors to make do-it-yourself coffee.

The Ny Carlsberg Glyptotek

MUSEUMS AND PLEASURE GARDENS

For a lovely day and evening of culture and fun, this is an excellent circular walk, taking in up to three art galleries and museums during the day and Tivoli, Copenhagen's historic pleasure gardens, in the evening.

DISTANCE: 1.5km (1 mile)
TIME: A full day
START: Ny Carlsberg Glyptotek
END: Tivoli
POINTS TO NOTE: It's easy to spend a day in the Glyptotek so keep an eye on the time if you want to visit the other museums as well.

NY CARLSBERG GLYPTOTEK

This tour begins on the steps of the **Ny Carlsberg Glyptotek** ❶ (Dantes Plads 7; www.glyptoteket.dk; Tue–Sun 11am–5pm; charge except Sun), a wonderful art gallery housing the collections of Carl Jacobsen (1842–1914), son of the founder of Carlsberg beer. His taste was predominantly for the ancient and classical, especially sculpture, and with his wife Ottilia, he built up one of the world's best collections of Egyptian, Greek, Roman and Etruscan art.

Jacobsen gave his collection to the nation in 1888 on the understanding that the state would create a suitable build-

ing for it. When the Glyptotek (derived from Greek and meaning 'a storage place for statues') first opened in 1897, it lay in open country with a view to the east across the swampy environs of the harbour. Jacobsen was not overly impressed, thinking it rather remote and inappropriately close to plebeian Tivoli. Much of the world-class modern collection showcasing the Impressionists, Post-Impressionists and Danish 19th-century art was built up after Jacobsen's death.

Level 1

As you pass through the impressive porticoed facade, you can see through to the grand, airy 19th-century **Winter Garden**, strewn with plants and statues and home to the museum's excellent café, see ❶. Directly ahead are the steps to level 2; at the far end on the left is the entrance to the modern extension.

Level 2

Level 2 is home to the **Greek and Roman Collections**, the **Egyptian collection** and **19th-century French** and **Danish sculpture**. Among many other treas-

The Greek and Roman collection at the Glyptotek

ures, including a whole room dedicated to **Rodin**, this is the place to come for an intimate picture of the faces of the past, including such notaries as Alexander the Great, his father Philip of Macedonia, the Roman emperors Caligula (still with traces of ancient paint on the face), Augustus and Hadrian. Don't miss the atmospheric Egyptian collection, which you enter down steps as if in to a tomb. Among the startling collection of artefacts are some wonderful sarcophagi plus painted models of tombs and scenes of Egyptian daily life.

The Modern Wing

The modern wing, designed by the architect Henning Larsen, houses a beautiful collection of **Etruscan and Mediterra-nean art** and an impressive **French collection**, which includes works by artists such as Gauguin, Degas, Monet, Manet, Bonnard, Van Gogh, Cézanne, Renoir, Pissarro and Berthe Morisot. Look out for Degas' statue of a 14-year-old dancer (1880–1), Manet's *Absinthe Drinker* (1859), Van Gogh's *Landscape from St Rémy* (1889) and Gauguin's *Skaters in Frederiksberg Gardens* (1884), dating from the time that he and his Danish wife and family lived in Copenhagen.

DANSK DESIGN CENTER

The **Dansk Design Center** ➋ (H.C. Andersens Boulevard 27–9; www.ddc.dk; charge), across the road, no longer has a

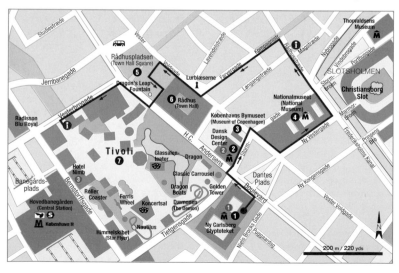

Ethnic masks at the National Museum

permanent exhibition, but check the website for upcoming design-related events. The striking building is the work of architect Lars Henning. There's also another good café here, the **Café Dansk**, see ❷.

MUSEUM OF COPENHAGEN

Walk down Stormgade to the **Museum of Copenhagen** ❸ (Københavns ByMuseet; Stormgade 20; www.copenhagen.dk; daily 10am–5pm; charge, under-17s free, Fri free), which was given an exciting boost when work began on the Metro system's new circle line. As the excavators moved in, all kinds of archaeological goodies came to light, some of which have changed the standard interpretations of Copenhagen's past. Expect to be taken from Copenhagen's early days as a small fishing village to modern times, via atmospheric reconstructions and interactive exhibits, as well as fascinating objects from the collection.

NATIONAL MUSEUM

The next port of call is the **National Museum** ❹ (National Museet; Ny Vestergade 10; www.natmus.dk; Tue–Sun 10am–5pm; free), Denmark's national cultural collection. At the end of Stormgade, take a right on Vester Voldgade and first left down Ny Vestergade. The museum is a little way down on the left.

The collection ranges from the prehistoric period to the modern day in Denmark and also includes a wonderful ethnographic collection. The ground floor is home to prehistory and the children's museum. The first to third floors can be confusing but the rooms all run around the atrium with ethnography, coins and medals, the Middle Ages and the state rooms on the first floor; the history of Denmark (1660–2000) and more ethnographic collections (including those of the Inuit) on the second floor; and Near Eastern and Greek and Roman antiquities on the third floor.

Ground Floor

The museum's amazing **prehistoric exhibition** includes unique archaeological treasures such as the **Gundestrup Cauldron**, thought to show scenes of human sacrifice and one of the world's few depictions of the Iron-age god Cernunnos; the **Trundholm Chariot of the Sun**, dating from *c*.1200 BC, when the Danes worshipped the sun, imagining it riding through the sky in a chariot pulled by a celestial horse; and the fascinating **Egtved grave** belonging to a blonde young woman wearing a string skirt, bodice, dagger and hairnet. A companion grave belongs to a young man with a full head of hair and rings in his ears.

First Floor

As you come up the stairs from the atrium, facing towards the street, the **Danish Middle Ages and Renaissance** is located on your left and an **ethnographic collection** on the right. The two collections are, in many ways, similar;

The bright lights of Tivoli

both vast, both charting the social and religious practices of a time and place, from minute articles to entire rooms and houses. (Both collections also continue directly above on the second floor.) Don't miss the **Royal Apartments** (Rooms 127–134), including the marvellous **Great Hall**, which date from the 1740s when the building was still a royal palace, home to the Crown Prince Frederik V.

The ethnographic collection on this floor includes artefacts from **Africa**, **India**, **Indonesia**, **New Guinea**, **Japan**, **China**, **Central Asia** and **Siberia** as well as a music room featuring world music and a fascinating slide presentation.

RÅDHUSPLADSEN

From the National Museum, turn left. At the bottom of Ny Vestergade you'll find the Frederiksholms Kanal and the island of Slotsholmen (see page 78). For Rådhuspladsen turn left again and third left onto Farvergade Kompagnistraede, home to the astronomer Tycho Brahe in 1597, until you come to **Rådhuspladsen ❺**.

The square, which dates from the end of the 19th century, is now a large space surrounded by hotels and restaurants. A new metro station is due to open here in 2017. Rådhuspladsen plays an active part in city life and is the site for Christmas and New Year festivities and concerts. It is dominated by the town hall or Rådhus, dating from 1905 after the town hall on Nytorv became too small for the city's needs. In front of it is the **Dragon's Leap Fountain**, likened to a spittoon at its unveiling in 1904: the addition of the dramatic bull in 1923 silenced the critics. Next to it the **Lurblæserne**, two bronze lur-blowers atop a 12-metre (40ft) column; local lore has it that the horns sound if a virgin walks past! Originally only one horn-player was planned for the monument, which explains the men's jostle for space.

Town Hall

The **Town Hall ❻** (Rådhus; Rådhuspladsen 1; tel: 33 66 25 82; Mon–Fri 9am–4pm, Sat 9.30am–1pm; free; tours in English Mon–Fri 3pm, Sat 10am) was built in mock-Gothic style by architect Martin Nyrop in 1905. A statue of Bishop Absalon and fantastical sea creatures adorn the facade. Inside, the entrance hall is a flurry of pseudo-Renaissance splendour with golden mosaics and a minstrels' gallery. Visitors can climb the 300 steps up the splendid **clock tower** (entry by tour only, Mon–Fri 11am and 2pm, Sat noon; charge) for an excellent view of the city and also see **Jens Olsens Verdensur** (Mon–Fri 9am–5pm, Sat 10am–1pm; free), which is said to have over 14,000 parts. It is the world's most accurate mechanical clock, with an estimated error of 0.4 seconds every 300 years! If it is sunny or you just need a place to sit down, there is a pretty **garden** (daily 10am–4pm) with benches behind the Town Hall. Walk down either side of the building and walk through the first open gateway that you reach.

The Town Hall   *Up, up and away in Tivoli*

TIVOLI

To visit the amusement park **Tivoli** ❼ (Vesterbrogade 3; ticket booking: 33 15 10 12; www.tivoli.dk; mid-Apr–late Sept daily 11am–late; also opens around Halloween and Christmas, see website for details; charge), cross H.C. Andersens Boulevard by the writer's statue to the entrance opposite.

Founded in 1843 outside the city walls, Tivoli is as popular now as it has ever been, entertaining over five million visitors every year. It has a great atmosphere, and there are plenty of rides for adults and kids alike. For the hardy, there are four roller coasters: the classic wooden **Rutschebanen** celebrated its 100th birthday in 2014, while **Dæmonen** is the most extreme coaster, looping the loop at speeds of up to 80kmh (50mph). The swing-and-spin **Aquila** whirls its victims through 360° at a stomach-lurching 160kmh (100mph). There are stunning views over the city from **Himmelskibet**, the tallest carousel in the world at 80 metres (260ft) high. The **dragon boats** on the lake, the **pantomime theatre**, the **Tivoli boys guard**, old-fashioned sidestalls, and trees and lakes all lit with Chinese lanterns have a romantic old-world charm for non-adrenalin junkies.

There is also lots of music and drama here: the **concert hall** is one of the best in Copenhagen offering ballet and opera (buy tickets in advance); the **open-air stage** sees loud, free rock and pop concerts every Friday night; and the pantomime theatre is free, as are the many musical groups playing on bandstands throughout the park. If you get peckish, there are over 40 eateries ranging from juice stalls and fast-food stands to top-end restaurants. Perhaps the best for a full Danish experience is **Grøften**, see ❸.

The Copenhagen Card (see page 132) allows for free admission. To go on any of the rides you need to buy a multi-ride pass (199dkk) or separate tickets (25dkk); rides need from one to three tickets each.

Food and Drink

❶ CAFE GLYPTOTEK

Tel: 33 41 81 28; Tue–Sun 11am–5pm; €–€€
Lovely salads and light lunch dishes but especially popular for its homemade cakes.

❷ CAFE DANSK

H.C. Andersens Boulevard 27–9; tel: 33 69 33 69; www.ddc.dk; Mon–Fri 9am–5pm; €
As you might expect, the café has been stylishly arranged by Danish designers. Soups, salads and sandwiches are good.

❸ GRØFTEN

Tivoli; tel: 33 75 06 75; www.groeften.dk; daily noon–10pm; €€€
Grøften has been here for 141 years, so it must be doing something right. It serves traditional Danish food straight from "grandma's kitchen" – *smørrebrod*, roast pork, fried fillet of plaice and apple pie.

SLOTSHOLMEN

Slotsholmen is the oldest site in Copenhagen for it was here, in 1167, that Bishop Absalon built a castle to protect the little fishing village of Havn from the unwanted advances of German pirates. A castle has stood here ever since and, 900 years later, the island is still the centre of national government.

DISTANCE: 2km (1.25 miles)
TIME: A full day
START: Palace forecourt
END: Black Diamond
POINTS TO NOTE: This route is not the most leisurely, packing in lot of sights, especially if you stop for lunch. It's a great day for busy sightseeing, though.

This is the fifth castle to stand on Slotsholmen (Castle Island). The first was a fortress surrounded by a limestone wall; it lasted 200 years before it was destroyed in 1367 by the Hanseatic League, a German alliance of trading guilds that monopolised trade in the Baltic and Northern Europe.

The second castle was built in 1375; in 1417 it gained in importance when the Danish king, Erik of Pomerania, made Kjøbmandehavn (now Merchants' Havn, reflecting its growing commercial success) his state capital. It was enlarged over the years but by the 18th century was falling down – something commented upon by visiting digni-

taries – and Christian VI, mindful of his position, razed it to the ground.

The third castle, a beautiful Baroque palace, was erected between 1731 and 1745 but it fell victim to fire in 1794 and only the magnificent stables and intimate red-and-gold theatre escaped the flames (see page 81). Homeless, the royal family repaired to the mansions of the aristocratic elite at Amalienborg from which they never returned (see page 47).

Between 1803 and 1828 a fourth castle, designed by the classical architect C.F. Hansen, was built. Used for ceremonial occasions and entertaining, in 1848 it, too, went up in smoke, with just the Palace Church and the Riding Ground left standing.

The fifth and current castle was built between 1907 and 1928 by Thorvald Jørgensen who, mindful of the fate of its predecessors, built its walls of reinforced concrete with granite facings. It is home to the State Rooms, the Folketinget (Parliament), Prime Minister's Office and Supreme Court.

The castle close-up

SLOTSHOLMEN IN A DAY

Before starting the tour of Christiansborg (www.christiansborg.dk), you may be interested in investigating some of the iconic buildings that you can see as you stand at the main gate of the castle. **Holmens Kirke ❶**, Holmens Kirke (Mon–Sat 10am–3.30pm; Sun noon-4pm; free), another of Christian IV's projects, lies across the water. It was originally a naval forge, where anchors were made, but was converted into a church for the navy in 1619. Queen Margrethe was married here in 1967.

Note, too, the fabulous building with the twisted spire, directly across the canal from the church. This is the **Stock Exchange ❷**, (Børsen; closed to the public but you can take a virtual tour at http://english.borsbygningen.dk), built in 1618–24 by Christian IV, who wanted to make Copenhagen a great trading centre. The building was constructed with many doors on a narrow dam with water on both sides, so that goods could be unloaded directly into the building from ships. It originally housed a sim-

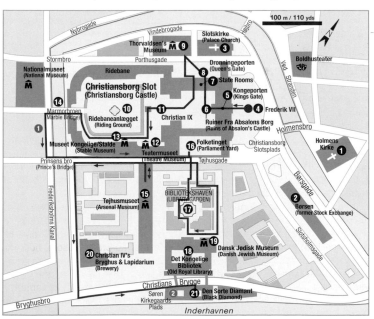

The impressive Throne Room

ple hall, which had storage space on the ground floor and booths and offices on the upper floor. In 1625, Christian enhanced the building by adding 18 gables and a 54-metre (177ft) spire, made up of four entwined dragons' tails, said to protect the building. The three golden crowns on top represent Denmark, Norway and Sweden. It did not become a stock exchange until the mid-19th century. The traders are now long gone, and the building is used as offices.

The neoclassical building with the portico to the north is the **Palace Church ❸** (Christiansborg Slotskirke, Christiansborg Slotplads; July daily 10am–5pm, rest of year Sun only; free), a lovely, light, airy affair, built by C.F. Hansen between 1813 and 1826 after its Rococo predecessor burnt down in 1794. Almost 200 years later, in June 1992, during Whitsun Carnival, it was beset by fire again, its cupola and dome crashing to the floor. It has now been restored to international acclaim.

The Ruins of Absalon's Castle

Now to start the tour proper. Take a look in the castle forecourt at the **equestrian statue ❹** by H.W. Bissen, which represents Frederik VII (1848–63), before passing through the **Kings Gate ❺**. Stop to visit the **ruins of Absalon's Castle ❻** (May–Sept daily 10am–5pm, Oct–Apr Tue–Sun 10am–5pm; charge), which will give you an idea of the size as well as the history of this site. As well as the remains of the walls, houses, a bakery and Absalon's chapel, you will be privy to Absa-

lon's 'secret', an ancient toilet, through which detritus washed into the harbour. Look out, too, for a wooden pipe, which was part of a system of hollowed-out tree trunks that brought fresh water to the castle from Lake Emdrup 6km (4 miles) away.

There are also some remains of the second castle, including the foundations of the terrible 'Blue Tower', in which prisoners, noble and plebeian alike, could be holed up for years. Princess Leonora Christina, a favourite daughter of Christian IV, spent almost 22 years locked up here after her husband Count Corfitz Ulfeldt plotted against the new king, Frederik III. Ulfeldt was accused of treason in 1663 but died before he could be executed.

The State Rooms

The **State Rooms ❼** (www.christiansborg.dk; daily 10am–5pm, closed Mon Oct–Apr; charge) are reached via the **Queen's Gate ❽**, which dates back to the time of the fourth palace. They are best visited on one of the recommended tours (in English 3pm; included in ticket price), which include the **Throne Room**, the **Dining Room**, the **Royal Chambers**, the **Great Hall** with tapestries by Bjørn Nørgaard, and the **Queen's Reference Library** lined with roughly 3km (2 miles) of shelving. The guides are so enthusiastic that if you weren't before, you are bound to be a royalist by the time you finish the tour.

Thorvaldsen's Museum

If you are interested in classical 19th-century sculpture, from here, walk

The Great Hall   *Costumes at the Theatre Museum*

through Prince Jørgens Gård bearing left to reach the **Thorvaldsen's Museum ❾** (Bertel Thorvaldsens Plads 2; www.thorvaldsensmuseum.dk; Tue–Sun 10am–5pm; charge, Wed free) on the far edge of the island, on Gammel Strand (see page 37). This brightly painted museum, its exterior depicting a life-size scene of the great sculptor's triumphant homecoming from Italy in 1838 after an absence of 40 years, houses virtually the entire collection of Bertel Thorvaldsen (1770–1844). His plans, casts, originals and replicas, plus his antiques – including examples of Egyptian, Greek, Etruscan and Roman works – and his collection of paintings, are all here. He is buried in the courtyard at the centre of the museum, which opened in 1848.

The Riding Ground
Back in the Inner Courtyard, look up at the tower that dominates the palace roofline; at 106 metres (348ft), it is one metre taller than the Town Hall and thus the highest in the old part of the city.

Now walk through to the **riding ground ❿**, which survived the fire of 1848. The equestrian statue, complementing the one in the palace forecourt, depicts **Christian IX ⓫** and is the work of sculptor, Anne Marie Carl Nielsen (1863–1945), wife of the Danish composer Carl Nielsen.

Theatre and Stable Museums
The Theatre and Stable Museums are under the arcade on the left-hand side of the riding ground. Both were part of the third palace and the sole survivors of the fire in 1794.

The **Theatre Museum ⓬** (Christiansborg Ridebane 18; www.teatermuseet.dk; Tue–Thu 11am–3pm, Sat–Sun 1–4pm; charge, under-18s free) is not to be missed. One of the oldest court theatres in the world, it was designed by the French architect Nicolas-Henri Jardin and has been restored to how it would have looked in its sumptuous heyday between 1767 and 1881, when it was a stage for opera and drama. On a dramatic note, it is here that Christian VII's powerful adviser Struensee was arrested for treason.

$50 Million Theft
Some 4.5 million books are a lot to keep track of as Frede Møller-Kristensen, an employee of the Royal Library's Oriental department, realised. Between 1968 and 1978 he removed 3,200 items, including manuscripts by Martin Luther and first editions by Immanuel Kant, Thomas More and John Milton. Møller-Kristensen sold over two million dollars' worth of books and remained undetected until his death in 2003. But his family were careless in selling the remainder and their cover was blown when books belonging to the library appeared at auction at Christie's in London. A police raid on the family house unearthed 1,500 books and they received sentences of between 18 months and three years each.

Canon at the Arsenal Museum

Enhanced with mannequins and music, visitors can wander backstage, through the boxes, and stand on the stage, surrounded by props and other memorabilia.

The **Stable Museum** ⑬ Christiansborg Ridebane 12; www.christiansborg.dk; July daily 10am–5pm; May, June, Aug and Sept daily 1.30–4pm; Oct–Apr Tue–Sun 1.30–4pm; charge) next door houses the collection of state coaches and carriages in palatial, marble-columned surroundings that kept the king's horses in equine splendour. An astonishing 250 horses were housed here in 1789; now there are about 15 of them, and they can occasionally be seen in their stalls.

The Arsenal Museum

Turn left and walk towards the Rococo **Marble Bridge** ⑭ (Marmorbroen). Built in 1744, it is the most ornate of the nine bridges linking Slotsholmen to the surrounding city districts: originally its pavements were of Norwegian marble. Cross over and have a bite at **Kanal Cafeen**, see ❶, or wait until you get to the Black Diamond.

For the **Arsenal Museum** ⑮ (Tøjhusmuseet; Tøjhusgade 3; Frederiksholmskanal; http://natmus.dk/toejhusmus eet; Tue–Sun noon–4pm; charge), cross the Marble Bridge, turn left and then left over **Prince's Bridge** (Prinsens Bro) into Tøjhusgade. About two-thirds of the way down on your right, the museum is housed in a splendid brick building dating from 1598, which used to be Christian IV's cannon hall. It's worth a visit

for the building alone – reputedly the longest in Europe at 163 metres (535ft) – not to mention the museum's staggering collection of weaponry ranging from inlaid duelling pistols to cannons. The ground floor bristles with guns and artillery, while the upper floor traces the history of Denmark's wars from 1500 to the present, as well as showcasing items from the museum's vaults, such as a spanking collection of uniforms from Tsarist Russia.

The Old Royal Library and the Danish Jewish Museum

Come out of the Arsenal and turn right down to **Parliament Yard** ⑯. If you're interested in eavesdropping on the sessions of the Danish Parliament (Folketinget; www.thedanishparliament.dk), they are open to the public; when parliament is not in session, there are free English tours of the building (July–mid-Aug Mon–Fri 1pm and Sun 1pm, rest of year Sun 1pm only). Otherwise, go through a door on your right where you will find an attractive **garden** ⑰, complete with pond and statuary (Søren Kirkegaard is on the right). At the far end is the **Old Royal Library** ⑱, dating from 1906.

The **Danish Jewish Museum** ⑲ (Holmens Kanal 2; www.jewmus.dk; June–Aug Tue–Sun 10am–5pm, Sept–May Tue–Fri 1–4pm, Sat–Sun noon–5pm; charge; under-18s free) charts the life of the Jewish community in Copenhagen from the 17th century, when immigrants were rather aristocratic, to just before

The Royal Library   *Stable Museum*

World War II, when lower-class sections of society began to arrive to escape the hardships of Eastern Europe. The exhibition does not cover the Holocaust; this is covered at the Frihedsmuseet (Resistance Museum; see page 51).

The museum is also remarkable for its stunning interior, by the architect Daniel Libeskind. The design comprises interlocking sections, many of which tilt to one side, which are intended as a metaphor for the amicable history of the Jewish community and the Danes.

The Lapidarium of Kings and the Black Diamond

Retrace your steps along Tøjhusgade, turning left before Prince's Bridge to walk alongside Frederiksholm Kanal. Towards the further end of the cobbled lane is the ivy-covered **Christian IV's Brewery** ⑳ (Bryghus), one of Copenhagen's oldest buildings. It was originally built as part of Copenhagen's fortifications before it was turned into a brewery to supply beer to the navy. Inside lies the **Lapidarium of Kings** (www.kongerneslapidarium.dk; daily 10am–5pm, closed Mon Oct–Apr; charge), a fascinating collection of 300 sculptures and statues. Gathered from parks and squares when they are in danger of becoming too damaged by the elements, some are restored and released back into the wild, while others are retired here permanently. Highlights of the collection include the equestrian statue of Frederik V from Amalienborg; and the collection of 18th-century Norwegian and Faroese peasants from the gardens of Fredensborg Palace.

Continuing your walk alongside the water brings you to the **Black Diamond** ㉑ (Den Sorte Diamant; Christians Brygge 1; www.kb.dk/en/dia; July–Aug Mon–Sat 8am–7pm, Sept–June Mon–Sat 8am–10pm; free), the modern extension of the Royal Library. It opened in 1999 and takes its name from its shiny black exterior and slanting silhouette. The library's archives include original manuscripts by H.C. Andersen, Søren Kirkegaard and Karen Blixen. It is also home to the National Museum of Photography (with regular temporary exhibitions) and the Queen's Concert Hall. If you haven't had lunch yet, head to **Søren K**, see ❷, on the ground floor.

The colourful canalside

CHRISTIANSHAVN AND HOLMEN

Christianshavn is one of the city's most colourful areas and the closest you will get to seeing how Copenhagen looked before the fire in 1728. It was created as a harbourside merchant town to help promote trade.

DISTANCE: 3km (2 miles)
TIME: A full day
START/END: Knippel's Bridge
POINTS TO NOTE: If you find yourself short of time, an appealing way to see some of Christianshavn is to take a harbour tour (see page 46).

Christian IV wanted to make Copenhagen the cultural, religious and business centre for the whole of the Nordic region and, as such, needed to enhance the naval and trading capabilities of the city.

Between 1618 and 1623, he had fortifications built in the swampy area between Copenhagen and the island of Amager. Five bastions were completed by 1623. By 1639 he decided that he wanted to build a town and gave the order for Christianshavn (Christian's Harbour) to be built, allowing for dockyards and warehouses alongside the merchant housing. He was so determined for this new city to be populated that he offered many of Copenhagen's wealthy merchants independence, free land, 12 years unrestrained by taxes and several other incentives to up sticks from their comfortable homes and business premises on the mainland and settle here instead.

His experiment worked and by the time he died in 1648, Copenhagen had become the naval and economic centre of the region.

CHRISTIAN'S CHURCH

Start at the green-towered **Knippel's Bridge ①** (Knippelsbro), the site of the first bridge between the mainland and Amager Island. Built in 1937, it is named after Hans Knipp, the tollkeeper of the first bridge erected in 1618. Note the six black, shiny buildings on your right, designed by the architect Henning Larsen, in stark contrast with the old-world atmosphere of the rest of the area. Walk up as far as Strandgade and take a right and walk down to Christian's Church.

Christian's Church ② (Christians Kirke; Strandgade 1; Tue–Fri

Canal boat　　　　　　　　　　　*Aerial view of Christianshavn*

10am–4pm; free) is one of two splendid churches on Christianshavn. It was built in 1754–9 by Nicolai Eigtved, Frederik V's master architect, who designed many of Copenhagen's 18th-century churches. This elegant rococo church is notable for its unusual, theatrical layout in which three tiers of seating galleries run around the walls, with the royal pew in the centre opposite the altar, technically in the position of the 'stage'. Originally named Frederiks Kirke, the church's name was changed in 1901 to reflect the importance of Christian IV. Today, it's also known as the Theatre Church, and is sometimes used as a concert venue, for example, during the Jazz Festival.

Outside the church, cross the road and walk down Johan Semps Gade to the waterside. To your left you will see the five ship-like masts of **Cirkelbroen** ❸, a beautiful pedestrian swing bridge designed by Danish-Icelandic artist Olafur Eliasson.

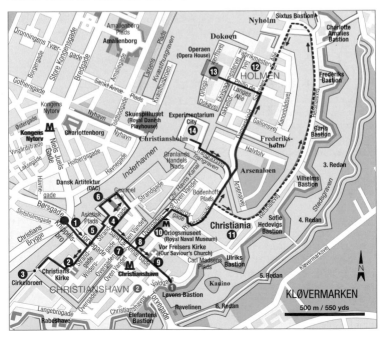

The view from Our Saviour's Church

STRANDGADE AND THE DOCKS

Walk back up to Torvegade and cross over into **Strandgade** ❹. This elegant 17th-century street was the one of the earliest, and **Nos 30** and **32** were the first houses to be built here. They originally had curved attic gables similar to those adorning Rosenborg Castle; these have since been replaced by an additional storey. The painter Vilhelm Hammershøi lived at No. 30 between 1899 and 1909, producing many of his trademark grey-tone interiors here.

As its name, Beach Street, suggests, Strandgade was originally right on the shoreline, with jetties and harbourside gardens. The closer to the water (and Copenhagen) you were, the smarter the address. It still has a certain cachet today: the 'world's best restaurant', Noma, lies at its furthest end.

Go through a wooden door on the left, opposite Sankt Annæ Gade, into **Asiatisk Plads** ❺. This is named for the Asiatisk Kompagnie, which traded with India and China from here in the 18th century. It was also responsible for commissioning and paying for the excessively expensive statue in the Amalienborg Plads (see page 47). On the north side, the marble façade of the elongated rococo warehouse was designed by Nicolai Eigtved in 1750 and dates from Christianshavn's heyday. It is now a conference centre.

Walk past the lovely old boats and bear right, past the end of the next building into **Gammel Dok** (Old Dock). On the far side

is the **Danish Architecture Centre (DAC)** ❻ (Dansk Arkitektur Center; Strandgade 27B; tel: 32 57 19 30; www.dac.dk; daily 10am–5pm, Wed until 9pm; charge; free Wed eve), Denmark's foremost exhibition centre for new architecture. Housed in a lovely old converted warehouse with exposed beams, it has constantly changing exhibitions. It also has a good bookshop and its café has an excellent waterside view. Further up on **Grønlands Handels Plads** opposite Nyhavn, the warehouses belonged to the Royal Greenland Trading Company (Kongelig Grønlandske Handel) and were used to store whale oil, skins and dried fish. There was then, and still is now, a Greenlandic population in Christianshavn.

Walk back down Strandgade to Sankt Annæ Gade; note **No. 32** on the corner of the junction, thought to be the oldest house in Christianshavn, dating from c.1622. Follow Sankt Annæ Gade to the two lovely cobbled streets overlooking the houseboats on the **Christianshavn Canal: Overgaden Neden Vandet** ❼ (Upper Street Below the Water) is on your left and **Overgaden Oven Vandet** ❽ (Upper Street Above the Water) on your right. Cross the bridge and head towards **Our Saviour's Church**, with the twisting, golden spire.

OUR SAVIOUR'S CHURCH

Our Saviour's Church ❾ (Vor Frelsers Kirke; Sankt Annæ Garde 29; www.vor frelserskirke.dk; daily 11am–3.30pm)

Christiania mural   *Our Saviour's Church tower*

is the oldest church in Christianshavn, built by Christian V for the inhabitants of the new harbour district between 1682 and 1694. Dedicated to Our Saviour, it is a wonderful example of Dutch Baroque style and is particularly well known for its spiralling tower (June–Sept Mon–Sat 10am–7.30pm, Sun 10.30am–7.30pm; Oct–Nov and Mar–May Mon–Sat 10am–4pm, Sun 10.30am–4pm; charge), which twists to a height of 90 metres (295ft). The view from the top of the external stairway is exhilarating but the climb is not for the unfit or acrophobic. The pine-wood structure almost seems to sway in strong winds and it closes to visitors in bad weather. Above you is a golden ball and a 3-metre (10ft) figure of Christ (reputedly the ugliest statue in Copenhagen!).

Inside is a light-filled, white-walled church with tall windows in the shape of a Greek cross. The cherub-covered font has a sad history: it was given by Frederik IV's childless, morganatic wife in 1702; she died in childbirth in 1704, and her baby died nine months later. The altarpiece, inspired by the altar in the Roman church of S.S. Domenico e Sisto, shows God (represented by the sun) and the events of Maundy Thursday, when Christ prayed that he should be spared the crucifixion.

Christian V's insignia can be seen on the entrance, the ceiling and the three-storey organ, which rests on two elephants, the emblem of Denmark's most prestigious order, founded in 1450. The Order of the Elephant was instituted in its current form in 1693 by Christian V. Royalty and heads of state may belong; the billionaire industrialist Mærsk Mc-Kinney Møller is the only living commoner to be a member. Nicolas Ceaucescu, late former Romanian dictator, is the only head of state to have had the honour revoked. The pulpit dates from 1773 and is decorated with figures of the apostles.

Turn left out of the church and walk to the end of the road; bear left up onto the fortifications, and on your right is one of Christianshavn's best restaurants, **Bastionen and Løven**, see ❶.

ROYAL NAVAL MUSEUM

Retrace your steps and walk down Overgaden Oven Vandet, passing the **Royal Naval Museum** ❿ (Orlogsmuseet; Overgaden Oven Vandet 58–64; www.orlogsmuseet.dk; Tue–Sun noon–4pm; free) on your right. Although there's little information in English here, there are some beautiful 17th-century model ships, as well as uniforms, nautical instruments and weapons. The long, rococo-style building was formerly used as a school, a prison, a hospital and then a rehabilitation centre for wounded naval personnel.

CHRISTIANIA

If you wish to visit **Christiania** ⓫, take Brobergsgade, the second right

Boats moored on the canal

after the Royal Naval Museum, and then keep walking until you end up on Prinsessegade. Opposite is the colourful mural-covered entrance to Copenhagen's 'Free State', a 19th-century, ex-army barracks that was taken over by freethinkers in 1971.

Christiania is home to just over 1,000 people, out of a population in Christianshavn of 9,000. To get the most out of it, take a tour (www.rundvisergruppen.dk; July–Aug daily 3pm, Sept–June Sat–Sun 3pm; charge 40dkk – take correct money); just wandering around can be a little underwhelming.

HOLMEN

From here retrace your steps and take a right up Prinsessegade. The quickest thing to do here is to wait for a No. 9A bus, which will take you up to near the **Opera House** on Holmen. Alternatively, take a right on to Refshalevej and walk up along some of the **bastions** though this will take you a good half hour at least.

Holmen ⑫ is made up of five man-made islands (Nyholm, Dokøen, Frederiksholm, Arsenaløn and Christiansholm, now connected by bridges), which were created from 1690 for the royal navy. It is built on muddy landfill that was dredged up by convicts who walked in huge treadmills in the waterway between Copenhagen and Amager. Eventually, the authorities supplied a horse-drawn dredger. Parts of the islands rest on ships that have been sunk and filled with boulders.

Nyholm, the first island, was built to replace the naval dock at Gammelholm, which had become too small and the water too shallow for the navy's fleet of ever-larger and faster ships. The **Sixtus Bastion** at its far end is still the place from which cannon are fired in salute, and there are several unique historical buildings still standing.

Once Holmen was a working naval base and its workers came across the water every day from Nyboder (see page 52). They were considered so important that during the plague in 1711–12, which killed a third of the population, they lived in huts on Nyholm to keep them away from infection.

The navy remained on Holmen for three centuries until it finally, and regretfully, closed its base in 1993. Since then, the area has seen an increase in public spaces and housing and is now also home to four art schools and the modern **Opera House** ⑬ (Operaen; Ekvipagemestervej 10; box office tel: 33 69 69 69; www.operaen.dk; charge for guided tours only). Opinions regarding its strikingly contemporary design (by Henning Larsen) vary, especially with regard to its controversial position on the 'Golden Axis' with the Amalienborg and the Marble Church on the other side of the harbour. But whatever the critics say, the building is impressive, standing 14 storeys high (five underground), with a flat grey roof that blends in with the sky.

The Opera House

Inside, a large glass-fronted foyer looks out over the water, lit by several huge, one-tonne lamps by artist Olafur Eliasson, who constructed them from thousands of pieces of glass that change colour depending on the temperature. In the centre, the main auditorium is encased in Canadian walnut and looks like a huge wooden pumpkin. Inside, it is a masterpiece of acoustic design, with an elaborate gold-leaf ceiling made of over 100,000 pieces of 23.75-carat gold.

The building took four years to build and was a gift to the nation by the A.P. Møller Foundation, established in 1953 by a wealthy Danish shipping magnate. The behind-the-scenes tour is very interesting; the areas you access depend on rehearsal schedules, but there are over 1,100 rooms in the building, so you won't be stuck for something to see. If you are lucky you will get to stand on the stage itself.

From here, hop on the 9A bus and go back to Knippel's Bridge; or, if you have bored children, hop off at **Experimentarium City ⑭** (Trangravsvej 12; www.experimentarium.dk; Apr–Oct daily 10am–5pm, Nov–Mar Mon–Fri 10am–4pm, Sat–Sun 10am–5pm; charge), instead. This hands-on interactive science centre is open while Experimentarium's main premises, north of Copenhagen in Hellerup, undergo a large-scale expansion. This square of land is officially called Christiansholm, but it is affectionately known as 'Paper Island' (Papirøen), so-called because the Danish press once stored their paper here! Their lease is up in 2017, after which the whole area is expected to undergo a major redevelopment.

Once back at Knippel's Bridge, if you enjoy being afloat, you could now see Christianshavn's canals from the water by hiring a rowing boat (as Copenhageners have done since the 19th century) from Christianshavns Bådudlejning & Cafe (Overgaden Neden Vandet; tel: 32 96 53 53; June–Aug 9am–midnight); or while away your time in the local shops and cafés, notably **L'Altro**, see ❷.

Food and Drink

❶ BASTIONEN AND LØVEN

Lille Mølle Christianshavn, Voldgade 50; tel: 31 34 09 40; www.bastionenloven.dk; Tue–Sun 11am–10pm; €–€€€
This charming restaurant is in an old mill on the ramparts of Christianshavn. It serves excellent Danish food and is especially popular for its weekend brunches (175dkk).

❷ L'ALTRO

Torvegade 62; tel: 32 54 54 06; www.laltro.dk; Mon–Sat 6pm–midnight (kitchen closes at 10pm); €€
Owned by the same brothers who own nearby Michelin-starred Era Ora, this offers excellent, traditional, home-made Italian food.

St James' church

ROSKILDE

Seaside Roskilde is a relaxing day out just 25 minutes away by train. It is considerably older than Copenhagen and for centuries was much more important. This walk takes you to the town's highlights, the cathedral and Viking Ship Museum, via ancient sights and then back through the park.

DISTANCE: 5km (3 miles)
TIME: A full day
START: Railway Station
END: Church of Our Lady
POINTS TO NOTE: If you are short of time, concentrate on the cathedral and the Viking Museum. Also note that restaurants serve lunch until about 3pm and don't serve again until about 5pm.

Roskilde is thought to have been founded in the 10th century by the splendidly named Harald Bluetooth (Harald I) of Denmark, a Viking who converted to Christianity c.AD 960. It is well placed at the bottom of a fjord, and tucked away but with access to the North Sea. Harald established his court here and also built a church on the site of the current cathedral.

By 1020, Roskilde was a bishopric, and in 1158, Bishop Absalon, who later founded Copenhagen, became bishop of Roskilde. He established several more churches and monasteries, until there were 14 parish churches and five con-

vents and monasteries in addition to a brick church on the site of the present cathedral. In the Middle Ages, Roskilde was one of the largest, most important cities in Northern Europe, with between 5,000 and 10,000 inhabitants and thousands of visiting pilgrims each year.

Today Roskilde is a quiet market town, woken up each year by the four-day **Roskilde Festival** (www.roskilde-festival. dk), which ranks alongside Glastonbury in the music calendar. Held on a site 3km (2 miles) south of the centre, Northern Europe's biggest festival attracts 130,000 paying punters and world-famous rock and pop artists such as Bob Dylan, Rihanna, Metallica, The Rolling Stones, Björk and the Arctic Monkeys.

TO THE CATHEDRAL

From the Italian-inspired station, which dates from 1847, turn right up Jerbanegade. The wall on your left encloses **Gråbrødre Kirkegård ❶**, an attractive church surrounded by a graveyard now used as a park, which stands on the site of a 13th-century complex belonging

The royal throne

to the Franciscans. Take a look at the beautiful view through the gates or turn left down Store Gråbrødretorvstræde if you want to enter the park.

Walk across cobbled **Hestetorvet** ❷, named for the horse market that was held here in the 12th century, just inside the ramparts by the eastern gate, where you cannot miss the **Roskilde Jars**. These are the work of artist Peter Brandes and stand 5 metres (16ft) high and weigh 24 tonnes. They were gifted to the city in 1998 on its 1,000th anniversary by a local firm, and, as they are both storage jars and urns, represent Life and Death.

Pass between the café and the pharmacy to the shopping street, **Algade** ❸, an ancient street that has been paved for over 700 years. Before you follow the route down Sankt Peders Stræde, wander along Algade to look at medieval paving just beyond the Hotel Prindsen; the imposing red-brick 17th-century apothecary's building; and the old merchant's house opposite at No. 9. There is a good family restaurant **Bryggergården**, see ❶, at No. 15; go through its archway to see the timbered backs of the old houses. Also, have a look through the gates of No. 31 to see the back of the Old Priory, which you will see shortly at closer quarters. Now turn down Sankt Peders Stræde until you reach **Roskilde Priory** on your right.

Roskilde Priory
Roskilde Priory ❹ (Roskildekloster; Sankt Peders Stræde 8; www. roskildekloster.dk), was built in 1565 in Dutch

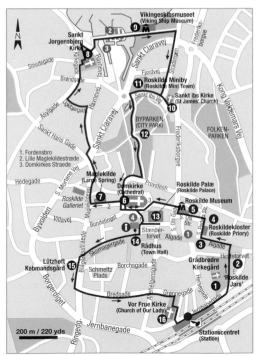

Intricate detail on the royal tombs

Renaissance style as a manor house. It stands on the site of a former medieval priory, which was destroyed during the Reformation in 1536 – its bricks were sold off and reused in many of Roskilde's buildings. Shortly after it was built, the manor house was bought by the widows of two Danish war heroes and run as a home for unmarried noblewomen: they lived in great style, as a tour of the Great Hall, abbey church and reception rooms will show. However, this is still a working monastery, and individual visitor access is restricted to tours, in Danish only, on Wednesdays in July at 11am and 2pm.

Tourist Office and Roskilde Museum

Out of the Priory, cross the road and walk down Sankt Ols Stræde; you can see the spires of the cathedral ahead of you. Keep walking straight on if you want to visit the tourist office **Visit-Roskilde** (Stændertorvet 1; tel: 46 31 65 65; www.visitroskilde.com; Mon–Thu 10am–5pm, Fri 10am–4pm, Sat 10am–1pm), which is based inside the Rådhus (town hall) on the corner of the main market square (**market days** are Wednesday and Saturday). Otherwise turn right at the end and head for **Roskilde Museum ⑤** (Sankt Ols Gade 18; www.roskildemuseum.dk; daily 11am–4pm; charge, under-17s free). The museum offers over 6,000 artefacts relating to the history of Roskilde and nearby Lejre, from prehistoric times until the 1970s.

THE CATHEDRAL

From here, cross over Sankt Ols Gade into Domkirkes Stræde. Turn left and pass in front of the cathedral for the main entrance; visit now or on your way back from the Viking Ship Museum.

The **Cathedral ⑥** (Domkirke; http://visit.roskildedomkirke.dk; Apr–Sept Mon–Sat 9am–4.45pm, Sun 12.30pm–4.45pm; Oct–Mar Tue–Sat 10am–3.45pm, Sun 12.30pm–3.45pm; closed during services; charge, under-17s free) is a Unesco World Heritage Site and one of the earliest brick-built buildings in Northern Europe. Pick up an information sheet on your way in so you have a plan.

Work on the church began in the 1170s, under Bishop Absalon, but the building was completed by his successor Peder Sunesøn, who was aware of the new Gothic style that was then emerging in France. (Indeed, this is one of the earliest Gothic buildings outside France.) The cathedral is famous for being the resting place of the 39 Danish kings and queens, going back to the Middle Ages; their chapels and tombs are a fascinating display of changes in style. There are also **pillar tombs** in the sanctuary behind the choir, of royals (including Harald Bluetooth) who were originally buried in the two, possibly three, earlier churches that have stood on this site.

Inside, you are greeted with a white, airy interior with bare brick columns, medieval frescoes and some Renais-

Chapel of the Magi　　　　　*The red-brick exterior of the cathedral*

sance furniture, including the pulpit, organ and altar. Before the Reformation in 1536, the nave would have been empty of pews or pulpit; instead there were 75 side chapels where mass was said daily for the souls of the dead. On your left, on the wall to the left of the west window, don't miss the **mechanical clock** with figures of St George and the Dragon that re-enact the dragon's defeat and death cries on the hour.

The frescoes in the **Chapel of the Magi** on the south side are some of the best and date from 1462. This is also where you'll find the unique 'King's Pillar', where visiting kings stood to be measured – Peter the Great's height marker is the highest by far. Opposite, on the north side, are two medieval chapels that were given startling new decorations in 2010. St Andrew's Chapel gained a glittering new altarpiece by artist Peter Brandes, while in St Birgitte's Chapel, you'll find a very modern sarcophagus, designed by Bjørn Nørgaard, which will eventually hold the present queen Margrethe and her husband. Get kids to hunt for the little green devil who, armed with pen and ink, is writing down the names of anyone who is misbehaving.

The oldest frescoes are found at the east (altar) end and were part of the pre-Reformation, Catholic side chapels. On the north side of the **ambulatory**, note the fresco depicting Bishop Absalon and a little further to the south, the tomb of the three-legged 'ghost horse', said to be jet black with blazing red eyes, the sight of which was an omen of one's impending demise.

The **choir** has an ornate Renaissance altar piece that features scenes from the New Testament. Also here is the tomb of Denmark's first queen regnant, Margrethe I – the little bells hanging from her clothing were all the rage in the 15th century. There are also some beautiful stalls, carved with scenes from the Old Testament on the south side and the New Testament on the north, with odd little trolls wandering through the narrative.

TO THE VIKING MUSEUM

Coming out of the cathedral, turn right, looking towards the sea. If time is pressing, you can take a direct route to the Viking Ship Museum from here by following the signs from Skolegade. Otherwise, cross Skolegade and head into leafy Lille Maglekildestræde. This takes you past the **Maglekilde** ❼ (Large Spring), on your right, inside a wooden well house that dates from 1927 and topped by an older mermaid weathervane. In the 19th century, this spring supplied water for five mills in industrialised Roskilde; it now yields one sixth of what it used to.

At the end of the road, turn right onto Maglekildevej, where you'll see the spring's water gushing out of the mouth of a head of Neptune. Walk past the **Roskilde Galleriet**, a commercial art gallery, until you reach Sankt Claravej, lined with 17th-century cottages. Turn

A replica Viking ship

right and first left on to Havnevej and then left again onto Uglebjergvej.

St Jorgensberg's Church

At the junction, turn right onto Asylgade, which then turns into the pretty Kirkegade, with **St Jorgensbjerg Church** ❽ (Sankt Jorgensbjerg Kirke; July–mid-Aug Mon–Fri 10am–noon; www.sjk.dk; free) on your right. This is Denmark's oldest intact stone building, with a choir and nave dating from the 11th century. Pop in if it is open; inside, there is a 19th-century votive ship model, a 16th-century crucifix and the remains of a 'leper's space' in the north wall, where people with leprosy received communion through a knee-high hole in the wall.

Walk through the churchyard, looking out over the lovely view of the fjord, and then down the steps until you come out on Havnevej. Turn right, then immediately left onto the harbourside, where you'll then see the wooden buildings of the **Viking Ship Museum** in front of you.

VIKING SHIP MUSEUM

Arguably the highlight of a trip to Roskilde is the excellent **Viking Ship Museum** ❾ (Vikingeskibsmuseet; Roskilde Harbour; www.vikingeskibsmuseet.dk; daily mid-May–Aug 10am–5pm, Sept–mid-May 10am–4pm; charge), passionately dedicated to Viking ships and sailing. The core exhibits are five well-preserved boats that were discovered in 1962 in the channel close to Skuldelev, 20km (12 miles) north of Roskilde. They had been deliberately scuttled – over a thousand years ago – to create an underwater blockade against raiders. The fragments were excavated and painstakingly jigsawed back together, to reveal a fishing boat, a coastal trader, an ocean-going trader and two fighting vessels – a *snekke* (the smallest type of Viking longship) and a great 60-oared warship.

As well as seeing the originals in the beautifully designed Viking Ship Hall, you can step aboard re-creations of the boats at the jetty, constructed in the museum's boatyard using traditional Viking methods and materials. You can also experience a Viking raider or trader's life for yourself by rowing out into the fjord in one of the evocative, creaking wooden ships (mid-May–Sept, sailing times vary; tel: 46 30 02 53 or see website for details; charge).

For lunch, there are two options, a restaurant boat, **MS Sagafjord**, see ❷, or the museum restaurant, **Snekken**, see ❸, near the entrance. If you have brought a picnic, there are several benches overlooking Roskilde's peaceful harbour, filled with white sails; and if the weather is not cooperating, there are also picnic tables inside the museum.

BACK TO TOWN

To take a different route back, turn left out of the museum. When you get to Strandengen, turn right and follow the road to the junction with Sankt Ibs Vej.

Viking coins

St James' Church ⑩ (Skt Ibs Kirke), a ruin with roots in the 12th century, stands on your left. Turn right and follow the road round untll you come to **Roskilde Mini Town** ⑪ on your right, another millennium gift to the town in 1998. The model shows Roskilde as it was in the 14th century.

Cross the road and enter the **City Park** ⑫ (Byparken), the site of various medieval archaeological remains, through a gate on your left. Walk up through the park for about 500 metres/yds, heading for the cathedral. It is easy to see its variety of architectural styles from this side. Don't forget to look back at the sea, with the ships' masts pointing skyward in the distance.

Walk round the cathedral into Domkirke Pladsen. If you haven't yet eaten, there is a nice little cellar restaurant, **Radhus Kaelderen**, see ❹, on the corner of Fordensbro.

Walk down Fordensbro into Stændertorvet, the main square, which was laid out as it is now in 1908. On your left stands the golden-walled **Roskilde Palace** ⑬ (Stændertorvet 3), a rather modest Baroque affair dating from the 1730s and built on the site of a medieval bishop's palace. Sections of the building are accessible to visitors, including the excellent **Museum of Contemporary Art** (Museet for Samtidskunst; http://samtidskunst.dk; Tue–Sun noon–4pm; charge; under-18s free), with two floors of changing exhibitions. It focuses on art from the 1950s onwards, with a particular interest in sound and video installations.

On the right is the **Town Hall** ⑭, dating from 1884. Note its splendid tower (c.1550), the only remaining part of the 12th-century church of St Laurentius. You can visit the **ruins** (May–Aug Mon–Fri 11am–4pm; charge) of the church, preserved under the square along with some items found during an archaeological dig.

BACK TO THE STATION

To return to the station, turn right out of the square down the shopping street Skomagergade. Continue to the end and take a left down Ringstedgade. On the right is **Lützhøft Købmandsgård** ⑮

Return to Dublin

The largest of the five Viking ships found in the fjord and now showcased in the Viking Museum is *Skuldelev 2*, a 30-metre (100ft), ocean-going warship that was originally built in Dublin c.1040. She was reconstructed between 2000 and 2004 and, named *Havhingsten fra Glendalough* (The Sea Stallion from Glendalough), set sail back to Dublin on 1 July 2007 with a crew of 70. The ship maintained an average speed of 2.5 knots with every second oar manned, and a top speed of 12 knots under sail. She arrived, seven weeks and 1,852km (1,000 nautical miles) later, on 16 August.

Roskilde Palace

(Ringstedgade 6–8; Apr–Dec Mon–Fri 11am–5pm, Sat 10am–2pm, closed Mon Jan–Mar), an old merchant's house with a charming shop that is reminiscent of the 1920s, and the Museum of Tools, with a collection from the period 1840–1950.

Keep on until you reach Bredgade. Turn left and carry on, crossing Allehelgensgade on to Grønnegarde. Turn right into Fruegade. The **Church of Our Lady** stands on your right.

Dating from the late 11th century, the **Church of Our Lady** ⑯ (Vor Frue Kirke; tel: 46 35 58 14) was an important,

wealthy church – so much so that St Margaret of Højelse, a relative of Bishop Absalon, was buried here in 1177. It was also connected to a Cistercian convent that was built close by in 1160. The convent was abolished in 1536, and its buildings and the eastern end of the church were demolished around forty years later. It has a pretty white-washed interior and the 17th-century pews were carved by Casper Luebbeke, Master of Roskilde.

Turn right out of the church and at the end, turn left onto Jernbanegade. The station is a little further along on your right.

Food and Drink

① RESTAURANT BRYGGERGÅRDEN

Algade 15; tel: 46 35 01 03; www.restaurantbryggergaarden.dk; Mon–Thu 10.30am–11pm, Fri–Sat 10.30am–midnight, Sun noon–midnight; kitchen open Mon–Sat 11am–10pm, Sun noon–9pm; €

Good solid food served up in a cosy pub-like

② MS SAGAFJORD

Roskilde Harbour; tel: 46 75 64 60; www.sagafjord.dk; Apr Thu–Sun 1–3pm and 6–9.30pm, May, June and Sept Tue–Sun 1–3pm and 6–9.30pm, Jul and Aug Tue–Sun noon–2pm, 3–4.30pm and 7–10.30pm; €€

Lunchtime buffet or evening menu of Danish specials, eaten while cruising in Viking waters along the Roskilde Fjord.

③ RESTAURANT SNEKKEN

Vindeboder 16; tel: 46 35 98 16; www.snekken.dk; daily 10am–9pm; kitchen open daily 11.30am–4.30pm and 5.30pm–9.30pm; €€–€€€

Café or restaurant meals in lovely, airy venue with views over the water. The New Nordic menu is heavily influenced by ingredients the Vikings would have used.

④ RADHUS KAELDEREN

Fondensbro 1; tel: 46 36 01 00; www.raad huskaelderen.dk; Mon–Sat 11am–11pm; €€

Good restaurant in the cellar of the town hall, with traditional Danish food. Seating in the small courtyard in summer.

Typical colour-washed houses

HELSINGØR

*Famous for its fictional association with William Shakespeare's Hamlet,
Helsingør (Elsinore) is a charming town on the banks of the Sound, just
6.5km (4 miles) away from Sweden across the water.*

DISTANCE: 3km (2 miles); further if visiting Technical Museum
TIME: A half/full day
START: Railway Station
END: Technical Museum
POINTS TO NOTE: You will need to do some careful planning to squeeze everything on this tour in. You may find it more convenient to do the tour In the opposite order.

Helsingør is an historic town, with entire streets of well-preserved, colour-washed buildings. Conveniently, the tourist office (Havnepladsen 3; tel: 49 21 13 33; www.visitnordsjaelland.com; June and July Mon–Fri 10am–5pm, Sat–Sun 10am–2pm; Aug Mon–Fri 10am–5pm, Sat 10am–2pm; Sept–May Mon–Fri 10am–4pm) is just across from the railway station: it sells the Copenhagen Card, which will get you into the town's museums.

From the tourist office, turn right along Strandgade (Beach Street) to **Skibsklarerergården** ❶ (Strandgade 91; http://helsingormuseer.dk; admission by tour only: Tue–Fri noon, 1pm, 2pm and 3pm; Sat 10am, 11am, noon and 1pm; Sun noon, 1pm, 2pm and 3pm; charge), a former grocers and ship chandlers, originally dating from the 16th century. If you are ready for lunch, go back along Strandgade to Bramstræde and turn right to Stengade, the main pedestrian street, which is full of restaurants; check out **Madam Sprunck**, see ❶. Alternatively, treat yourself to an ice cream at **Brostræde Fløde Is**, see ❷, on Brostræde, one of several narrow streets that connect Strandgade and Stengade. This small establishment has been serving ice creams since 1922.

MARITIME MUSEUM OF DENMARK

Walk down to Havnegade. Turn left and walk round the dock in the direction of the castle, cutting along the pathway in front of the glass Culture Yard (Kulturværftet). The classic view of the castle's copper turrets is so revered

Castle detail

that the **Maritime Museum of Denmark** ❷ (Museet for Søfart; Ny Kronborgvej 1; http://mfs.dk; July–Aug daily 10am–5pm, Sept–June Tue–Sun 11am–5pm; charge) was built underground around the old port's dry dock in order to preserve it. Dedicate a couple of hours to the museum's absorbing collection, which does a fine job of illustrating Denmark's seafaring history; although the artefacts are somewhat outshone by the unconventional architecture.

KRONBORG CASTLE

Follow the path across the inlets and moats to **Kronborg Castle** ❸ (Kronborg Slot; www.kronborg.dk; June–Aug daily 10am–5.30pm; Apr, May, Sept and Oct daily 11am–4pm; Nov–Mar Tue–Sun 11am–4pm; charge), a magnificent Renaissance-style edifice and famous as the model for Shakespeare's 'Elsinore' in *Hamlet*. It was originally built in 1420 as a fortress to protect the town and to encourage trading ships to pay King Erik V the 'Sound Dues' that he demanded for sailing in these waters. Today it is a Unesco World Heritage site, with highlights that

include the ornate chapel, an immense banqueting hall, the King's Tapestries in the Little Hall, and some suitably miserable dungeons containing the slumbering Danish hero Holger Dansk.

SANKT ANNA GADE

Head back onto Havnegade, taking a right up Kongensgade and then first left in Sankt Anna Gade, an ancient street of much historical interest.

Carmelite Priory and City Museum

On your left is the **Carmelite Priory** ❹ (Karmeliterklosteret; Sankt Anna Gade 38; www.sctmariae.dk; mid-May–mid-Sept Tue–Sun 10am–3pm, mid-Sept–mid-May Tue–Sun 10am–2pm), a fine building dating from the mid-15th

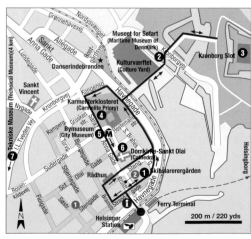

Spectacular Kronborg Castle

century. Its church (St Maria's/Sankt Maria Kirke) is decorated with recently restored frescoes dating from 1480–90, and the splendid Baroque organ dates from 1662–3.

Next door, in another priory building erected in 1516 as a sailors' hospital, the **City Museum** ❺ (Bymuseum; Sankt Anna Gade 36; Tue–Fri and Sun noon–4pm, Sat 10am–2pm; charge) has an interesting history, a Renaissance banqueting hall on the first floor and a mix of exhibits.

The Cathedral

Continue down the street and one block on on the same side you will see Helsingør's red-brick Gothic **cathedral** ❻ (Helsingør Domkirke; Sankt Anna Gade 12; www.helsingoerdomkirke.dk; May–Aug Mon–Sat 10am–4pm, Sept–Apr Mon–Sat 10am–2pm).

Originally a small Romanesque church dating from c.1200, this was the first church in Helsingør. The current building dates from 1559 and was made a cathedral in 1961. It contains a particularly fine 15th-century crucifix, a Renaissance pulpit (1568) and an exuberantly carved wooden altarpiece, decorated with gold leaf.

Technical Museum

It's worth heading to the far end of town for the **Technical Museum** ❼ (Danmarks Tekniske Museum; Fabriksvej 25; www.tekniskmuseum.dk; Tue–Sun 10am–5pm; also Mon

during school holidays; charge), which is full of captivating vehicles, gadgets and appliances, including more than 30 aeroplanes. Some of these belonged to Jacob Ellehammer (1871–1946), who designed and flew his own aeroplane in 1906, making him one of the first European pilots.

To reach the museum from Helsingør station, catch bus No. 802 in the direction of Espergærde and ask the bus driver to stop at Fabriksvej; the stop is right outside the museum.

Food and Drink

❶ MADAM SPRUNCK
Bramstræde 5; tel: 49 26 48 49; kitchen opens daily 11am–9.30pm; €–€€
This charming café-restaurant is housed in a half-timbered building dating from 1781. Light Danish and international meals are on offer during the day, with more expensive fare in the evening. You can eat out in the courtyard in summer.

❷ BROSTRÆDE FLØDE IS
Brostræde 2; tel: 49 21 35 91; open Apr–Oct; €
Denmark's oldest ice cream parlour serves a small, but delicious range of flavours. Ask for cream, jam and *flødeboller* (chocolate-coated marshmallow) for a real treat. Cash only.

The Louisiana Modern Art Museum

ART TOUR

There are three world-class art galleries outside Copenhagen that it would be a pity to miss. With time, planning and a willingness to walk, you can combine two of them in one trip.

DISTANCE: n/a
TIME: A full day
START: Ørdrupsgaard
END: Louisiana
POINTS TO NOTE: These are not the easiest places to combine as public transport isn't direct, but it is possible if you time it properly. Try to do the trip Tue–Fri if you can, as Louisiana stays open until 10pm then. If you want to check timetables and routes, visit www.rejseplanen.dk.

ØRDRUPGAARD

Just 8km (5 miles) out of Copenhagen, this is perhaps the only trip when a car would be handy. Otherwise, put your walking boots on. The best way to **Ørdrupgaard ❶** (Vilvordevej 110, Charlottenlund; www.ordrupgaard.dk; Tue and Thu–Fri 1–5pm; Wed 1–9pm; Sat–Sun 11am–5pm; charge) is to take the S-tog or the regional Kystbanen line to Klampenborg Station (20 mins), then take bus No. 388 to Vilvordevej (5 mins). If you pre-

fer to walk the 2.5km (1.5 miles) from the station, go down the stairs from the platform and turn left out of the station. Follow the road for about 250 metres/yds, turn left onto Christiansholmsvej, then right onto Klampenborgvej. After about a mile, turn left onto Vilvordevej. An alternative is to take the S-tog to Lyngby, then bus No. 388 to Vilvordevej.

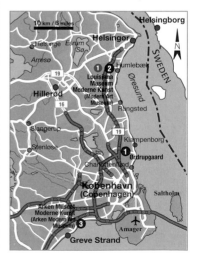

Henry Moore sculpture   *Ørdrupgaard entrance*

Ørdrupgaard is a lovely old house with a striking modern extension, full of Danish and European Impressionist paintings, with lots of premier-league artists, including Cézanne, Degas, Manet and Monet. There is also a delightful collection of paintings by Danish artist Vilhelm Hammershøi. Allow yourself plenty of time to tour the collection, as the free audio guide is thorough, and there is a pretty garden and a pleasant café. Design fans should also take a look at the house (Sat–Sun 11am–4.45pm) of visionary Danish furniture designer and architect Finn Juhl (1912–89), which borders Ørdrupgaard park and is part of the museum.

LOUISIANA

Walk (or take bus No. 388) to Klampenborg station. From here, take an S-tog to Humlebæk (direction Helsingør). The journey takes about 25 minutes, and then it's a 20-minute, signposted walk.

The wonderful **Louisiana Modern Art Museum ❷** (Gammel Strandvej 13,

Humlebæk; www.louisiana.dk; Tue–Fri 11am–10pm, Sat–Sun 11am–6pm; charge) is a work of art in itself. Several parts are buried into the hilly slopes, so you'll descend underground only to pop out unexpectedly into the sunlit sculpture garden. Glass walls blur the boundaries between art and nature, and you will find yourself as aware of the beautiful landscape outside as you are of the art inside.

The impressive permanent collection features work by artists including Arp, Francis Bacon, Calder, Dubuffet, Max Ernst, Sam Francis, Giacometti, Kiefer, Henry Moore, Picasso, and Warhol. The excellent **café**, see ❶, overlooking the Sound is a great place to have dinner.

Food and Drink

❶ LOUISIANA CAFE
Gammel Strandvej 13; Tue–Fri 11am–9.30pm, Sat–Sun 11am–5.30pm; €–€€
Sit by the fire in winter or by the water in summer. This pleasant café serves snacks and sandwiches all day, with a hot-and-cold buffet at lunch and in the evening.

Arken

In a marvellous building in the shape of a ship's hull, the **Arken Modern Art Museum ❸** (Arken Museet for Moderne Kunst; Skovej 100, Ishøj; www.arken.dk; Tue and Thu–Sun 10am–5pm, Wed 10am–9pm; charge) provides an ideal setting for the avant-garde works of art displayed here. The museum's permanent collection includes a room dedicated solely to Brit-Art heavyweight Damien Hirst. The museum's surroundings are being excavated so that it will eventually sit on its own island. To get there, take the S-tog to Ishøj (direction Hundige or Køge, 25 mins), and then bus No. 128; or the signposted walk takes 20 to 30 minutes.

DIRECTORY

Hand-picked hotels and restaurants to suit all budgets and tastes, organised by area, plus select nightlife listings, an alphabetical listing of practical information, a language guide and an overview of the best books and films to give you a flavour of the city.

Hotel Alexandra

ACCOMMODATION

Copenhagen's hotels tend to belong to national and international chains, and offer excellent facilities and decent if rather bland rooms. There are many hotels within a short walk of the city's main sights around Hovebanegård (Central Station): cheaper options tend to lie to the west in Vesterbro and more expensive ones around Rådhuspladsen. There are also several smart hotels around Kongens Nytorv and Nyhavn. A little bit out of the way, but with good views over the water, are the newer hotels on Kalvebød Brygge, south of Slotsholmen. Alternatively, head slightly away from the tourist centre and stay near Rosenborg or Amalienborg: Copenhagen's transport is so good that nowhere is far from the city centre.

Early bookings via the internet are usually cheaper than official rack rates. However, it is always worth ringing up to find out if a hotel can give you an even better deal; they may be able to if business is slow. This especially applies to places that are dependent on weekday business travellers, who may be willing to sweeten a deal with great weekend rates for couples, or themed packages that might include tickets to Tivoli or the opera.

If you're staying one week or longer, renting an apartment is a practical and economic option. The tourist office has a free booking service (tel: 70 22 24 42; Mon–Sat 9am–4pm) – see the accommodation section of www.visitcopenhagen.com for details.

Note that the metro system is currently undergoing a major extension, with 17 new stations due for completion in 2019. Naturally this involves a lot of construction noise (usually between 8am to 5pm). If this is a concern, check the schedule of works on the metro's website (www.m.dk/cityringen) or consult your hotel.

Tivoli and Radhusplådsen

Cabinn City

Mitchellsgade 14; tel: 33 46 16 16; www.cabinn.dk; S-tog: Hovedbanegård; €

There are four of these budget hotels in Copenhagen (see also page 110). Space is limited (many rooms have bunk beds) but this particular hotel is superbly situated, just a short walk from buzzing Tivoli. All-inclusive breakfasts (70dkk) are healthy and copious.

> Price for a standard double room for one night without breakfast in high season:
> €€€€ = over 2,000dkk
> €€€ = 1,500–2,000dkk
> €€ = 1,000–1,500dkk
> € = under 1,000dkk

Nimb's lavish exterior   _A cosy fireplace at Nimb_

Danhostel Copenhagen City

H.C. Andersens Boulevard 50; tel: 33 11 85 85; www.danhostel.dk/copenhagencity; bus: 5A; €

With over 1,000 beds, this five-star youth hostel is in a great location with far-reaching views. It's modern, comfortable, and the family rooms (accommodating up to 6 people) are extremely good value. Purchase an international YHA card to take advantage of the cheapest prices.

First Hotel Kong Frederik

Vester Voldgade 25; tel: 33 12 59 02; www.firsthotels.com; bus: 6A; €€€

Situated close to Rådhuspladsen and Tivoli, this historic hotel retains a classic 'English' atmosphere in its communal areas, while bedrooms are more Scandinavian, done out in a dusky palette of blacks, greys and creams. Rooms can get rather warm in summer.

Hotel Alexandra

H.C. Andersens Boulevard 8; tel: 33 74 44 44; www.hotelalexandra.dk; bus: 6A; €€€€

This environmentally-conscious retro hotel occupies a renovated apartment block dating from the 1880s. It is stylishly decorated in 1940s and 50s Danish style, with Arne Jacobsen furniture, Kaare Klint chairs and Poul Henningsen lighting. It's worth paying extra to stay in one of the 13 'Danish Design' rooms.

Hotel Danmark

Vester Voldgade 89; tel: 33 11 48 06; www.hotel-danmark.dk; bus: 10; €€

Located next to Rådhuspladsen, this hotel offers rooms furnished in subdued Scandinavian style. It's slightly tired, but is clean, cheap and carbon-neutral, and very peaceful for such a central location.

Imperial Hotel

Vester Farimagsgade 9; tel: 33 12 80 00; www.imperialhotel.dk; S-tog: Vesterport; €€€

A few minutes' walk from Rådhuspladsen and Tivoli Gardens, this modern hotel is more prepossessing on the inside than on the outside, with well-appointed, spacious rooms, plus fine restaurants and on-site parking.

Nimb

Tivoli, Bernstorffsgade 5; tel: 88 70 00 00; www.nimb.dk; S-tog: Hovedbanegård; €€€€

A romantic's dream, Nimb is located in inside Tivoli gardens. Its 17 fabulous boutique rooms contain a blend of modern and antique furniture, including four-poster beds, and the sleek bathrooms come with bathtubs and double sinks. Fourteen have working fireplaces that add to the romance in winter.

Radisson Blu Royal Hotel

Hammerichsgade 1; tel: 33 42 60 00; www.radissonsas.com; S-tog:

Scandic Copenhagen

Vesterport, Hovedbanegård; €€€€
Copenhagen's most iconic hotel was designed by architect and designer Arne Jacobsen. Although only one room (606) retains his original decor, the building as a whole has a nice retro/modern feel. Its excellent Alberto K restaurant has fabulous views over the city. Rates are generally lower at weekends, when weekday business guests leave.

Scandic Copenhagen

Vester Søgade 6; tel: 33 14 35 35; www.scandichotels.com; S-tog: Central Station; €€€€
A comfortable, centrally placed, sky-scraper hotel that looks out over Copenhagen's reservoirs and the Tycho Brahe Planetarium: binoculars are provided to admire the view. It also has a decent restaurant, a lobby bar and a gym.

Scandic Palace Hotel

Rådhuspladsen 57; tel: 33 14 40 50; www.scandichotels.dk; bus: all Rådhuspladsen buses; €€€€
Another hotel in the Scandic chain, this imposing historical landmark sits right on Rådhuspladsen. Public areas retain their old-world, Victorian grandeur while the comfortable, good-sized rooms are decorated in neutral Scandic style.

The Square

Rådhuspladsen 14; tel: 33 38 12 00; www.thesquare.dk; bus: all Rådhuspladsen buses; €€€
Stylishly decorated, this design hotel sits right on the City Square – its executive rooms overlook the hustle and bustle. Rooms are good-sized and comfortable, and the sixth-floor breakfast room has great city views.

Wakeup Copenhagen

Carsten Niebuhrs Gade 11; tel: 44 80 00 00; www.wakeupcopenhagen.com; S-tog: Hovedbanegård; €€
This budget hotel, designed by Kim Utzon, has small, sharp and crispy clean rooms containing flatscreen TVs and free Wi-fi. Prices rise as you go higher up the building – the 'Wakeup Heaven' rooms on the top floor have the best views. Its sister hotel, Wakeup Borgergade, close to Kongens Have, is a little nicer but less central.

Strøget and Around

Ascot Hotel

Studiestræde 61; tel: 33 12 60 00; www.ascot-hotel.dk; S-tog: Central Station; €€€
Set in a distinguished old bathhouse building in the Latin Quarter, this hotel offers suites, some with kitchenettes. Rooms are a little hit-and-miss: some are fresh and stylish, while others need a makeover. Very central and no traffic noise.

Hotel Kong Arthur

Nørre Søgade 11; tel: 33 11 12 12; www.kongarthur.dk; S-tog: Nørreport; €€€

Hotel d'Angleterre bar   *The spa at Hotel d'Angleterre*

Slightly off the beaten track beside Peblinge Sø, Kong Arthur has attractive rooms around a pretty inner courtyard. Its friendly Danish atmosphere makes it rightly popular with returning guests. Some suites have Jacuzzis, and treatments are available from the hotel's excellent spa.

Hotel Sankt Petri

Krystalgade 22; tel: 33 45 91 00; www.hotelsktpetri.com; S-tog: Nørreport; €€€€

'Bespoke' is a word that applies to virtually everything in this five-star hotel; from the original artworks on the walls to the orchids and designer modern decor. The bathrooms are stunning. Facilities include a respected restaurant, buzzing bars and an attractive summer terrace.

Ibsens Hotel

Vendersgade 23; tel: 33 13 19 13; www.ibsenshotel.dk; S-tog: Nørreport; €€

In the same group as Kong Arthur, and a near neighbour, this comfortable three-star hotel makes a virtue of its Tiny rooms, aimed at guests who are happy with a (cutely designed) 10 sq metres (108 sq ft) space; while people who like to sprawl will love the charming top-floor X-Larges.

Kongens Nytorv and Nyhavn

Best Western Hotel City

Peder Skramsgade 24; tel: 33 13 06 66; www.hotelcity.dk; metro: Kongens Nytorv; €€€

Located in an elegant town house, the City has an international feel, clearly expressed in its striking modern decor. It has a hospitable and friendly atmosphere – nothing is too much trouble for the staff – and does a good breakfast buffet.

Copenhagen Strand

Havnegade 37; tel: 33 48 99 00; www.copenhagenstrand.dk; metro: Kongens Nytorv; €€€

This cosy three-star hotel can be found on a side street just off Nyhavn in a converted warehouse dating from 1869. Its decor is slightly rustic yet modern and brings to mind its maritime position and history.

Hotel d'Angleterre

Kongens Nytorv 34; tel: 33 12 00 95; www.dangleterre.dk; metro: Kongens Nytorv; €€€€

This grand palace is indisputably Copenhagen's finest, a refuge for the wealthy and the beautiful. It's also the only hotel in Copenhagen with its own Victorian palm court! Facilities include an upmarket restaurant, spa, fitness centre and heated pool.

Hotel Bethel Sømandshjem

Nyhavn 22; tel: 33 13 03 70; www.hotel-bethel.dk; metro: Kongens Nytorv; €€

In a striking red-brick building with a turret, Hotel Bethel is a welcoming budget place. Half of its basic-but-

A room at Babette Guldsmeden

clean rooms look out over the canal, and the hotel hides Denmark's only sailors' church – ask at reception for a tour.

Hotel Opera

Tordenskjoldsgade 15; tel: 33 47 83 00; www.hotelopera.dk; metro: Kongens Nytorv; €€€

This is another charming three-star belonging to the Arp-Hansen group. Located on a side street close to the Royal Theatre on Kongens Nytorv, this English-inspired hotel dates from 1869. Rooms are comfortable but vary in size, as do the beds.

71 Nyhavn Hotel

Nyhavn 71; tel: 33 43 62 00; www.71nyhavnhotel.com; metro: Kongens Nytorv; €€€

Based in two former Nyhavn warehouses, which were once used to store spices from the Far East. The atmosphere is one of upmarket rusticity and many original features remain. Rooms are tiny but characterful; some have harbour views. The Pakhuskælderen restaurant is recommended for its tasty seasonal menu.

The Royal District

Adina Apartment Hotel

Amerika Plads 7; tel: 39 69 10 00; www.adina.eu; bus: 26; €€€

Situated 2.2km (1.4 miles) out of the centre, but very handy for cruise ships at the ferry terminal. A super spot, Adina consistently gets positive reviews for its splendid air-conditioned apartments, with bedroom, lounge, kitchenette and balcony. Facilities include a gym, sauna and small pool.

Babette Guldsmeden

Bredgade 78; tel: 33 14 15 00; www.guldsmedenhotels.com; bus: 1A; €€€

Babette is another gorgeous addition to the family-run Guldsmeden mini-chain. It sits apart from its siblings (see page 109) in the upmarket Royal District, but the atmosphere is similarly warm and welcoming. Suite guests have free access to the rooftop lounge and spa; others pay 125dkk.

Copenhagen Admiral Hotel

Toldodgade 24–8; tel: 33 74 14 14; www.admiralhotel.dk; metro: Kongens Nytorv; €€€€

Every room is different at this fabulous warehouse conversion, a stone's throw from Nyhavn. Original beams and designer teak furniture lend the hotel a rustic air, while the enormous galley-like lobby has naval memorabilia and model ships on view. It's also home to a very good French-inspired restaurant, SALT.

Phoenix Copenhagen

Bredgade 37; tel: 33 95 95 00; www.phoenix copenhagen.dk; bus: 1A, 66; €€€

This is an elegant hotel in a 17th-century

Scandic Front Hotel　　　　　*Exposed beams at the Admiral Hotel*

mansion, close to the Royal Palace and Kongens Nytorv. All rooms and suites are air-conditioned and furnished in the French Louis XVI style, although some are starting to look a little frayed at the edges.

Scandic Front Hotel
Skt Annæ Plads 21; tel: 33 13 34 00; www.scandichotels.com; metro: Kongens Nytorv; €€€

A comfortable representative of the Scandic chain. Families are welcome and some rooms have stunning views of the Opera House. Split-level suites come with top-of-the-range coffee-making machines. The location is usually quiet, but external building work is schedule until late 2015 – contact the hotel for details.

Rosenborg and Around

Hotel Christian IV
Dronningens Tværgade 45; tel: 33 32 10 44; www.hotelchristianiv.dk; www.hotelchristianiv.dk; €€€

A small, pleasant hotel located beside the lovely King's Garden (Kongens Have). Rooms are neat and bright, and fitted with modern Danish furniture; some quieter rooms overlook the inner courtyard. Complimentary coffee, tea, fruit and cake available.

Vesterbro and Frederiksberg

Absalon Hotel
Helgolandsgade 15; tel: 33 24 22 11; www.absalon-hotel.dk; S-tog: Central Station; €€€€

The decor in this family-run place features warm, wood tones and high-end fixtures and fittings, including giant HD TVs and organic bath products.

Andersen Boutique Hotel
Helgolandsgade 12; tel: 33 31 46 10; www.andersen-hotel.dk; S-tog: Central Station; €€€

One of the most delightful choices in Vesterbro, Andersen has small but brightly coloured and impeccably clean rooms. There are some nice extra touches, such as mini-fridges in the rooms and an evening Wine Hour so guests can mingle.

Axel Guldsmeden
Helgolandsgade 11; tel: 33 31 32 66; www.hotelguldsmeden.dk; S-tog: Central Station; €€€

This lovely place is one of four Guldsmeden hotels in Copenhagen; the company prides itself on its socially responsible, eco-friendly, organic credentials. Distinctive rooms are decorated with Balinese furniture in colonial style, and breakfasts are delicious. Axel has four stars, a more central location than Bertrams and Carlton (see below), and a spa and sauna.

Bertrams Guldsmeden
Vesterbrogade 107; tel: 70 20 81 07; www.hotelguldsmeden.dk; bus: 6A; €€€

Carlton Guldsmeden
Vesterbrogade 66; tel: 33 22 15 00; www.hotelguldsmeden.dk; bus: 6A; €€

Axel Guldsmeden's luxurious spa

Both hotels belong to the same chain as Axel Guldsmeden. They are just as cosy, but these two are further away from the city centre down Vesterbrogade: a bus or cab will be appealing if you have had a long day. Bertrams is particularly charming, with great service and a pleasant courtyard garden.

Best Western Hotel Hebron

Helgolandsgade 4; tel: 33 31 69 06; www.bestwestern.com; S-tog: Central Station; €€€

Hotel Hebron makes a decent base for exploring Copenhagen: staff are helpful and rooms agreeable, it's just 300 metres/yds from the gates of Tivoli, and the excellent buffet breakfast will set you up for a day of sightseeing.

Cabinn Express

Danasvej 32–34, Frederiksberg; tel: 33 21 04 00; www.cabinn.dk; metro: Forum; €

Cabinn Scandinavia

Vodroffsvej 55, Frederiksberg; tel: 35 36 11 11; www.cabinn.dk; metro: Forum; €

Both of these hotels in the functional, budget Cabinn chain are located close to Peblinge Sø (Lake), a 10-minute walk from Rådhuspladsen. You can sleep a family of four for under 1,000dkk. (See also Cabinn City, page 104.)

Copenhagen Crown

Vesterbrogade 41; tel: 33 21 21 66; www.copenhagencrown.dk; bus: 6A; €€€

This fresh, modern hotel has amenities for business travellers as well as holidaymakers. Most of the rooms look onto an inner courtyard, so street noise is less of an issue here than in equally central hotels.

Copenhagen Island

Kalvebod Brygge 53; tel: 33 38 96 00; www.copenhagenisland.com; S-tog: Dybbelsbro; €€€

You'll find this stylish place east of Vesterbro on an artificial island. It offers all mod cons, including a lovely restaurant, fitness centre with harbour views and sleek, chic rooms. Book well ahead, and a double can cost under 1,000dkk.

First Hotel Mayfair

Helgolandsgade 3; tel: 70 12 17 00; www.firsthotels.com; S-tog: Central Station; €€€

This early 20th-century hotel is a satisfying choice, just five minutes from the city's heart. Some rooms are small, but all are nicely decorated in boutique-hotel style; the same sense of design pervades the public areas too. Clean, cosy atmosphere and good service.

Hotel Avenue

Åboulevard 29; tel: 35 37 31 11; www.avenuehotel.dk; bus: 2A, 12, 66, metro: Forum; €€

Sitting on the border of Frederiksberg and Nørrebro, this funky little

design hotel has cosy rooms, a generous breakfast buffet and friendly staff. The lounge (a perfect example of Danish *hygge*) is perfect for relaxing. Represents great value for money in an expensive city.

Hotel Tiffany

Colbjørnsensgade 28; tel: 33 21 80 50; http://hoteltiffany.dk; S-tog: Central Station; €€

Hotel Tiffany is a small family-run hotel offering pleasant accommodation. There's no restaurant, but each room contains a practical kitchenette. You can't beat the prime location, close to Central Station.

Hotel Sct Thomas

Frederiksberg Allé 7; tel: 33 21 64 64; www.hotelsctthomas.dk; bus: 6A, 26; €€€

A friendly and good-value budget option, with bright rooms and a decent breakfast buffet. Make sure you book through the hotel website to get free Wi-fi (otherwise there is a charge).

Marriott Copenhagen

Kalvebod Brygge 5; tel: 88 33 99 00; www.marriott.com/cphdk; bus: 30; €€€€

A standard-issue Marriott in a decent location a short walk from Tivoli, with all the mod cons and perks that you would expect from a five-star hotel. Make sure to ask for a room overlooking the harbour.

Christianshavn

CPH Living

Langebrogade 1C; tel: 61 60 85 46; www.cphliving.com; bus: 5A; €€

One of Copenhagen's most unusual accommodation options, CPH Living is a purpose-built floating hotel with a splendid design aesthetic. The twelve style-savvy rooms on this converted barge have floor-to-ceiling windows so you can enjoy the harbour views; and in fine weather, there's a fabulous sun deck too.

Copenhagen Airport

Crowne Plaza Copenhagen Towers

Ørestads Boulevard 114–118; tel: 88 77 66 55; www.crowneplaza.com; €€€€

This place has super-sleek rooms and amazing views over Amager (especially at night). Careful environmental consideration went into its construction – it contains Denmark's first groundwater-based heating system and the largest solar panels in Scandinavia. A free shuttle bus runs to the airport.

Hilton Copenhagen Airport Hotel

Ellehammersvej 20; tel: 32 50 15 01; www.hilton.com; €€€

Directly linked to Terminal 3, this five-star hotel is perfect if you have an early-morning flight. It also has the largest rooms in the city, plus a swimming pool and a spa and wellness centre.

Caviar at Restaurant Koefoed

RESTAURANTS

Copenhagen has around 2000 restaurants, which are scattered all over the city, often in the most unlikely of places. The old butcher's district Kødbyen has a dense cluster of bars and restaurants and is a lively spot at night. The quiet residential streets of Christianshavn/Holmen seem to hold a higher-than-normal number of top-class restaurants, including Noma, Rene Redzepi's world-famous Nordic kitchen. Otherwise, you can pick and choose your eating place according to what district you're in and what your purse can bear.

Fifteen restaurants in Copenhagen have Michelin stars, and almost as many were awarded a Bib Gourmand for top-class dining at a more affordable price. Many restaurants have fixed-price menus: the greater the number of courses, proportionately the cheaper your meal becomes. If you are on a budget, eat in a café where a couple of unpretentious courses will set you back around 200dkk, or try out the *pølsevogn* sausage vans found all over town.

The Danes love their meat. In a city stuffed with restaurants, there are hardly any places that cater solely to vegetarians. The vegetarian and vegan menu at Botaniq (see page 117) is highly recommended, while Ambrosias Have (see page 121) does a tasty and reasonably priced vegetarian buffet. There are also several raw-food cafés where you can eat super-healthy lunches and some of the city's top restaurants will rustle up a meat-free alternative if given advance notice.

Note that Copenhagen's restaurants generally take a well-earned rest on Sundays (and some also on Mondays), so if you are wishing to eat out, check first that your chosen eating-place is actually open.

Tivoli and Rådhuspladsen

A Hereford Beefstouw

Tivoli, Vesterbrogade 3; tel: 33 12 74 41; www.a-h-b.dk; daily 11.30am–4pm and 5–10.30pm; €€€

A chain with a difference: long-standing favourite A Hereford Beefstouw invests a percentage of its profits into quality artworks that adorn its restaurants. Juicy steaks and seafood dishes are cooked to order, while an on-site brewery provides glasses of frothy beer.

Prices for an average three-course meal without wine:
€€€€ = over 550dkk
€€€ = 400–550dkk
€€ = 250–400dkk
€ = under 250dk

Fine dining at Formel B

Grøften

Tivoli; tel: 33 75 06 75; www.groeften.dk; noon–Tivoli closing time, kitchen closes 9.30pm; €€

A Tivoli stalwart since 1874, serving traditional food to generations of Danes. Come here for open sandwiches at lunchtime, or to sample its speciality dish, a beetroot borsch. It's big but cosy, and is run with smiling efficiency and real kindness to kids.

Kahler i Tivoli

Tivoli; www.kahler-i-tivoli.com; tel: 53 73 84 84; Sun–Thu: noon–11pm, Fri–Sat until midnight; €€€

Visitors to Tivoli are a captive audience, and food tends to be rather expensive for what you get, although Kahler serves decent enough meals considering the milieu. Best experienced at lunchtime, when you can eat *smørrebrød* on the sunny terrace.

Nimb

Berstorffsgade 5; tel: 88 70 00 00; www.nimb.dk; €€€

The wonderful Moorish Palace in Tivoli, built in 1909, contains three restaurants: the family-friendly brasserie (€€€), a Bar'n'Grill (€€€) serving steaks and cocktails, and the Terrace (€€€), a French-inspired bistro.

Vesterbro and Frederiksberg

Fiasco

Gammel Kongevej 176, Frederiksberg; tel: 33 31 74 87; www.fiasco.dk; Tue–Sat 5.30–10pm; €€

This rustic, unpretentious Italian restaurant offers borderline gourmet dishes at very reasonable prices. In the summer you can eat alfresco. Reservations recommended, as it's a cosy little place and very popular.

Foderbrættet

Vesterbrogade 41; tel: 33 23 64 63; http://foderbraettetkbh.dk; Mon–Wed noon–midnight, Thu noon–1am, Fri–Sat noon–2am; €

If you thought hotdogs were fairground food, think again. Fodebrættet has elevated this humble foodstuff to gourmet status, with delicious spices and toppings such as tzatziki or cabbage-and-mango. Sound comical, but it was voted Copenhagen's Best New Restaurant in 2014. Drinks list of cocktails or champagne.

Formel B

Vesterbrogade 182, Vesterbro; tel: 33 25 10 66; www.formel-b.dk; Mon–Sat 5.30pm–midnight, last table reservation at 10pm; €€€€

A charming Michelin-starred restaurant where you can relax in a restful white, chocolate and taupe interior. The menu changes every two weeks and offers dishes such as Danish cod with watercress, dandelion and cod roe; monkfish with snails, mushrooms and basil; and escalope of foie gras with kale and giblets. Summer terrace for outdoor dining.

Mielcke & Hurtigkarl's romantic dining room

Kødbyens Fiskebar

Flæsketorvet 100, Vesterbro; tel: 32 15 56 56; kitchen daily from 5.30–11pm; €€
This fashionable bistro, with its chic urban interior and mesmerising jellyfish tank, serves superb fresh fish and shellfish from the surrounding sea: poached cockles, Limfjorden oysters and blue mussels, cod from the Kattegat and razor clams.

Mielcke & Hurtigkarl

Frederiksberg Runddel 1; tel: 38 34 84 36; www.mhcph.com; Tue–Sat dinner only; €€€€
This experimental gourmet place is located in the beautiful rose gardens of Frederiksberg Park. The intimate interior is great for romantic dinners, but the terrace is the place to be on a fine day. The restaurant has its own herb garden which informs the ever-changing tasting menu.

Mother

Høkerboderne 9-15; tel: 22 27 58 98; www.mother.dk; Mon–Sat 11am–1am, Sun 11am–11pm, kitchen open Mon–Sat until 11pm, Sun 10pm €
Mother is one of the best-value restaurants in the cool Kødbyen area. It serves scrumptious sourdough pizzas, made in Neopolitan style, to hungry crowds. Reservations are only taken up to 8pm, then it's a free-for-all.

Neighbourhood

Istedgade 27; tel: 32 12 22 12; kitchen open Sun–Thu 5.30–10pm, Fri–Sat until 11pm; €
This fabulous Vesterbro pizza place serves organic pizzas made with half the normal amount of dough but at least twice the flavour. Innovative toppings include pumpkin sausage, garlic-roasted Argentinian giant shrimp, and chilli salami. Communal seating and a young cheery vibe.

Nose2Tail

Flæsketorvet 13A; tel: 33 93 50 45; Tue–Thu 5.30–midnight, Fri–Sat until 1am; €€
Hidden in a vaulted, white-tiled cellar in Copenhagen's former butchers' district, Nose2Tail has an appropriately meaty menu (free-range and organic, naturally): think pork crackling, juicy sausages and lamb steaks. Large, shareable meat-and-cheese platters let you try bits of everything.

Paté Paté

Slagterboderne 1; tel: 39 69 55 57; Mon–Wed 8am–midnight, Thu 8am–1am, Fri 8am–3am, Sat 10am–3am, Sun 10am–midnight; €€
Cosy, candlelit Paté Paté is a sociable place to dine. Spanish and Moroccan dishes, including plates of tapas, are served at big shared tables. You can stop by for a breakfast croissant, but with its bistro feel and huge winelist, it really comes into its own at night.

Restaurant Klubben

Enghavevej 4; tel: 33 31 40 15; kitchen

Dessert at BROR   *The kitchen at Marv & Ben*

open daily noon–9.45pm; €
This pub is a little too rough and ready to tempt tourists not already in the know. Sit at a wobbly table with plastic tablecloth and enjoy the huge portions of traditional home cooking, such as *frikadeller* with creamed cabbage and beetroot or the traditional Danish herring plate.

The Latin Quarter, Strøget and Around

BROR
Skt. Peders Stræde 24A; tel: 32 17 59 99; www.restaurantbror.dk; Wed–Sun 5.30pm–midnight, last reservation at 9.30pm; €€
No Noma reservation? No worries! BROR is run by a couple of Noma graduates. It serves a set four-course menu (two appetizers, main, dessert; 375dkk) of beautifully prepared and colourful food – flavours are light and subtle – on quirky mismatched china.

Det Lille Apotek
Store Kannikestræde 15; tel: 33 12 56 06; www.detlilleapotek.dk; kitchen open daily 11.30am–10pm; €€
The 'Little Pharmacy' is Copenhagen's oldest cellar restaurant, with crooked walls and antiques. It claims many writers as former customers, including Hans Christian Andersen and Ludvig Holberg and serves hearty Danish fish and meat dishes. Students love it.

Green Sushi
Grønnegade 28; tel: 33 11 88 99; daily 4–10pm; €€€
An excellent and cosy little place selling Japanese sushi, made from ingredients that have been farmed or fished using sustainable principles. There's an attached takeaway with a good-value set lunch If you want to eat on the move.

House of Souls
Vestergade 3; tel: 33 91 11 81; http://houseofsouls.dk; Sun–Wed 5–11pm, Thu–Sat 5pm–midnight; €€
If you grow weary of *smørrebrød* and *stegt flæsk*, a plateful of Caribbean soul food might give you the spice you're seeking. Tasty and unusual dishes include seafood gumbo, blackened catfish, jambalaya and Creole lime mousse.

Kobenhavner Cafeen
Badstuestræde 10; tel: 33 32 80 81; kitchen open daily 11.30am–10pm; €
This small restaurant has an old-time atmosphere and a traditional menu to go with it; *flæskesteg* (roasted pork, a Christmas speciality), *frikadeller* (meatballs), grilled plaice and a recommended cold table and daily two-person 'Plate' of marinated salmon, herring, shrimp, meatballs, vegetables and baked bread for 225dkk.

La Galette
Larsbjørnsstræde 9; tel: 33 32 37 90; www.lagalette.dk; Mon–Sat noon–4pm and

5.30–10pm, Sun 1–10pm; €

If *smørrebrød* and meatballs are beginning to pall, how about something complete different? Family-friendly La Galette sells delicious savoury and sweet crepes, prepared by a genuine Frenchman. Wash them down with a cup of crisp, dry Breton cider.

Marv & Ben

Snaregade 4; tel: 33 91 01 91; www.marvogben.dk; Tue–Sat 6–10pm; €€

This Nordic gastropub takes a great deal of pride in producing succulent, flavour-packed dishes based on seasonal ingredients: duck breast with chestnuts and sorrel, haddock served with cockles and a smidgen of seaweed, or juicy slow-roasted pork.

Oliver and the Black Circus

Teglgårdstræde 8A; tel: 74 56 88 88; http://oliverandtheblackcircus.com; Tue–Sat 5.30pm–1am; €€€

Crazy name, crazy place: Oliver's has a fabulous atmosphere and is full of quirks, from the decor – black walls, bare bricks and rams head – to the food. Gorgeous gourmet dishes (with six to choose from) contain unusual ingredients and flavours such as wood sorrel, pumpernickel and liquorice.

Riz Raz

Kompanistræde 20; tel: 33 15 05 75; www.rizraz.dk; daily 11.30am–midnight; €

This attractive Mediterranean restaurant is very popular and offers an excellent and varied vegetarian buffet. The cuisines of Lebanon, Morocco and Italy are all inspirations. There are some meat dishes for the more carnivorous.

Tight CPH

Hyskenstræde 10; tel: 33 11 09 00; www.tight-cph.dk; Sun–Thu 5–10pm, Fri–Sat 5–11pm; €€

One of Copenhagen's most beloved restaurants. Tight offers attractive raw-brick and warm wood surrounds, a lively international atmosphere, and some great grub: try the mussels and crab cakes for starters, followed by surf 'n' turf or a rack of juicy barbecue ribs, glazed in maple syrup.

Kongens Nytorv, Nyhavn and Around

Nyhavns Færgekro

Nyhavn 5; tel: 33 15 15 88; www.nyhavns faergekro.dk; kitchen open Sun–Thu 10.30am–10pm, Fri–Sat 10.30am–11pm; €–€€

Based in the old White Star Line office (of Titanic fame), the Færgekro is an unpretentious restaurant set in an 18th-century building. It serves good traditional food, and is especially popular at lunchtime for its *smørrebrød* and a good herring buffet.

Restaurant Koefoed

Landgreven 3; tel: 56 48 22 24; www.restaurant-koefoed.dk; kitchen open

Stylish cellar restaurant AOC

Tue–Sat noon–3pm and 5.30–9.30pm; €€€€

The classy, slow-food menu specialises in food from the Danish island of Bornholm. Diners are treated to fish prepared in Allinge's famous smokehouses, beer from the Svaneke brewery and Bornholm cheeses. Enquiring minds ask, "Where is its Michelin star?". Five-course tasting menu (600dkk).

The Standard

Havnegade 44; tel: 72 14 88 08; http://thestandardcph.dk; €€–€€€€

The old Art Deco hydrofoil terminal was converted by gastronomic entrepreneur Claus Meyer into three fabulous restaurants and a jazz club in 2013. Almanac serves modern Danish cuisine (lunch and dinner daily; €€€); light and airy Verandah has tasty pan-Indian dishes (Tue–Sat 5.30–9.45pm; €€); while former Noma chef Torsten Vildgaard mans the Michelin-starred Studio (Tue–Thu 6pm–midnight, Fri noon–3pm and 6pm–midnight, Sat 6pm–midnight; €€€€).

Umami

Store Kongensgade 59; tel: 33 38 75 00; www.restaurantumami.dk; kitchen open Mon–Thu 6–10pm, Fri–Sat until 11pm; €€€€

This stylish Japanese-French fusion restaurant is a popular celebrity haunt. There is a ground-floor cocktail bar and a sushi restaurant upstairs serving dishes such as ginger-poached duck breast with gyoza, sesame and garlic; and grilled veal tenderloin with wasabi and truffle sauce.

Rosenborg and Around

Ankara

Krystalgade 8; tel: 33 15 19 15; http://ankaracity.dk; Mon–Sat 11am–midnight, Sun 1pm–midnight; €

Extensive Turkish buffet-style eatery adapted for Danish tastes. In a city of expensive restaurants, the evening buffet here is a bargain at 119dkk. It also has two other premises, at Vesterbrogade 35 and 96.

AOC

Dronningens Tværgade 2; tel: 33 11 11 45; www.restaurantaoc.dk; Tue–Sat 6pm–1am; €€€€

Voted one of the world's top 50 restaurants, AOC is situated in a beautiful vaulted 17th-century cellar dining room. The New Nordic Kitchen five-, seven- or 10-course tasting menus change with the seasons: a typical dish might be venison with black trumpet mushrooms and fermented parsnip.

Botaniq

Frederiksborggade 26; tel: 33 36 33 30; daily 11am–8pm; €€€

One of only two 100 percent meat-free restaurants in Copenhagen, Botaniq is located in pleasant café-style premises near the Botanical Gardens and offers a small menu of vegan dishes, such as lentil bake with grilled apricots, roasted celeriac ravi-

The industrial interior at Amass

oli, and white chocolate ganache flavoured with fennel.

Kokkeriet

Kronprinsessegade 64; tel: 33 15 27 77; www.kokkeriet.dk; Mon–Sat 6–9pm; €€€€

This charming, relaxed modern restaurant boasts one Michelin star and a six-course set menu offering beautifully presented, interesting food combinations: scallops in buttermilk, with cabbage and malt; foie gras giblets, apples and cowberry; and carrot ice cream with lychee and liquorice. You can also eat à la carte and arrange to take lessons from the chef.

Kong Hans Kælder

Vingårdstræde 6; tel: 33 11 68 68; www.konghans.dk; Mon–Sat 6–10.30pm; €€€€

Set in Copenhagen's oldest building, mentioned in medieval texts. In the 19th century, Hans Christian Andersen lived in its garret. The food is French-influenced with an emphasis on simplicity and fresh ingredients and features roasted langoustines with black salsifys; glazed turbot with rosehip and *marjolaine*; and foie gras with local apples and Danish apple balsamic vinegar.

Pluto

Borgergade 16; tel: 33 16 00 16; www.restaurantpluto.dk; kitchen open Tue–Thu 5.30pm–10pm, Fri–Sat until 11pm; €€

A great place to go for a relaxed night out with lots of little dishes to swap and share. The food is Nordic tapas, best experienced in the good-value 12-course tasting menu (450dkk).

Restaurant Godt

Gothersgade 38; tel: 33 15 21 22; www.restaurant-godt.dk; Tue–Sat 6pm–midnight, closed July; €€€€

Godt means 'good', something of an understatement for this family-run, 20-seat gastronomic restaurant. The cuisine is European with daily four- and five-course seasonal menus; the wine list is mainly French. Reservations are advised.

Restaurationen

Møntergade 19; tel: 33 14 94 95; www.restaurationen.com; kitchen open Tue–Sat 6–10pm; €€€€

Multiple award-winning Restaurationen has survived for over 20 years in the upper echelons of Copenhagen's competitive dining world. It was the city's first bistro, serving Danish cuisine with French and Italian twists. The menu is revised weekly to incorporate local seasonal produce.

San Giorgio

Rosenborggade 7 (near the Kultorvet); tel: 33 12 61 20; www.san-giorgio.dk; Mon–Sat 6–11pm, kitchen closes 10pm; €€€

Nicely decorated with white-washed walls, dark wood furniture, chandeliers, candles and crisp white tablecloths, San Giorgio offers authentic Italian (specifically, Sardinian) cuisine

that is very much more than just pizza and pasta. Three fixed menus give you a choice on price.

Amalienborg and Around

Le Sommelier

Bredgade 63–65; tel: 33 11 45 15; www.lesommelier.dk; Mon–Thu noon–2pm and 6–10pm, Fri noon–2pm and 6–11pm, Sat 6–11pm, Sun 6–10pm; €€€

A charming French restaurant, Le Sommelier reputedly has the largest wine cellar in Denmark. The food is delicious (approach the *assiette tout chocolat* with an open waistband). The menu changes but expect high-quality lamb, beef, pork, duck and fresh fish dishes.

Madklubben Bistro de Luxe

Store Kongensgade 66; tel: 33 32 32 34; www.madklubben.info; Mon–Sat 5.30–10pm; €

If you want to dine out in Copenhagen in civilised style but don't have a bottomless wallet, try this relaxed and unpretentious spot. It keeps costs low by offering a basic (but high-quality) menu, with surcharges for more luxurious items such as lobster and smoked duck.

Rebel

Store Kongensgade 52; www.restaurant rebel.dk; tel: 33 32 32 09; kitchen open Tue–Sat 5.30–10.30pm; €€€

Halfway between Amalienborg and Rosenborg, Rebel offers delicious food, an excellent wine list and informal but attentive service. There's a

tasting menu (must be pre-ordered), or choose from the list of savoury and sweet "servings". Each costs 119dkk and four are recommended for a satisfying dining experience.

Slotsholmen and South of Strøget

Rio Bravo

Vester Voldgade 86; tel: 33 11 75 87; www.riobravo.dk; Mon–Sat 11.30pm–5am, Sun 5pm–5am; €–€€

This popular place is a favourite among late-night revellers. It's a no-nonsense, cowboy-style steakhouse, where even the seats at the bar are saddles. The kitchen stays open until 4am daily.

Slotskælderen

Fortunstræde 4; tel: 33 11 15 37; Tue–Sat 11am–3pm; €–€€

This is one of Copenhagen's most famous traditional lunch restaurants, dating from 1910 and much favoured by politicians from the nearby parliament. Enjoy their excellent open sandwiches and Danish menu, including home-cured herring and home-brewed *snaps*.

Sorgenfri

Brolæggerstræde 8; tel: 33 11 58 80; kitchen open Mon–Sat 11am–8.45pm, Sun noon–5pm; €

This 150-year-old *frokost* restaurant, tucked in a basement just north of Christiansborg Castle, is a good old-fashioned choice. It provides a very Danish

Edible flowers at Noma

experience of *smørrebrød*, beer and snaps, plus other traditional dishes like fried plaice, roast pork and meatballs served with red cabbage.

Tårnet

Christiansborg Slot; tel: 33 37 31 00; http://taarnet.dk; Tue–Sun 11.30am–4pm and 6–9.30pm; €€€

Lcoated in the tower of the Danish Parliament, this is one of the more unusually-sited of Copenhagen's restaurants. Try to get a table by the window for great city views. The modern Danish menu uses local produce and changes with the seasons.

Christianshavn and Holmen

Amass

Refshalevej 153; tel: 43 58 43 30; www.amassrestaurant.com; Fri–Sat noon–4pm (last seating 2pm), Tue–Sat 6pm–midnight (last seating 9pm); €€€€

Since opening in 2013, Matt Orlando's cutting-edge restaurant, housed in a converted warehouse, has been repeatedly tipped as a possible successor to Noma. It subscribes to New Nordic Kitchen principles, growing many of its own veggies, and has a laidback graffiti-decorated, trip-hoppy vibe. Harbour bus no. 991 or 992 stops nearby.

Era Ora

Overgaden Neden Vandet 33B; tel: 32 54 06 93; www.era-ora.dk; Mon–Sat lunch noon–3pm, dinner 6.30pm–midnight (kitchen closes 10.30pm); €€€€

This friendly Michelin-starred, stylish Italian restaurant by the canal has a calming, Italianate, beige-and-white interior and a pretty summer courtyard. Era Ora serves innovative cuisine with Umbrian and Tuscan roots, and is one of the best restaurants in the city.

No. 2

Nicolai Eigtvedsgade 32; tel: 33 11 11 68; www.nummer2.dk; Mon–Fri noon–2pm, Mon–Sat 5.30–10pm; €€€

From the same stable as gourmet restaurant AOC, this relaxed Nordic bistro offers a seasonal menu centred around Danish produce. You choose four dishes from the menu, such as mallard with kale, pan-fried brill or sea buckthorn with rosehip and salt caramel. Harbour bus no. 991 or 992 drops you right outside the door.

Noma

Strandgade 93, Christianshavn; tel: 32 96 32 97; www.noma.dk; €€€€

Noma is the stuff of legends, topping the S.Pellegrino World's 50 Best Restaurants list in 2010, 2011, 2012 and 2014. Superstar chef René Redzepi takes inspiration from Denmark, Iceland, Greenland and the Faroe islands, conjuring up up dishes such as bouillon of birch wine and mushrooms, chickweed and egg yolk; and reindeer and celery, woodruff and ramson onion capers, and has earned two Michelin

Sleek Danish design at Geranium

stars. Bookings are taken up to three months in advance; competition for a table is fierce.

Viva

Langebrogade kaj 570; tel: 27 25 05 05; www.restaurantviva.dk; Tue–Sat from 5.30pm; €

Moored by the Langebro bridge, this floating restaurant serves Mediterranean-inspired food with beautiful harbour views. It's a great spot for a romantic dinner – try to get a table on the top deck.

Nørrebro and Østerbro

Ambroslas Have

Nordre Fasanvej 230; tel: 21 85 16 77; www.ambrosiashave.dk; lunch daily 11am–3pm; €

The city's only shoe-free restaurant, peaceful Ambrosia has a super-cheap set buffet (125dkk) of seasonally-changing soups, mostly vegan mains and salads, served with homemade bread. Food is prepared using principles drawn from Ayurveda, macrobiotics and yoga.

Geranium

Per Henrik Lings Allé 4; tel: 69 96 00 20; http://geranium.dk; Thu–Sat noon–3.30pm, Wed–Sat 6.30pm–midnight, kitchen closes at 1pm and 9pm; €€€€

The proud bearer of two Michelin stars, Geranium is a little out of the way, situated on the 8th floor of a sports stadium overlooking Fælledparken. It's well worth the journey: perfect food, perfect wine, perfect service.

KiinKiin

Guldbergsgade 21; tel: 35 35 75 55; www.kiin.dk; Mon–Sat 5.30–9pm; €€€€

The name means 'come and eat!', a hard offer to turn down. This is the first Asian restaurant in Denmark to win a Michelin star, offering a modern Thai five-course menu in a lovely ambience. Romantics should book Table 9, the most private corner.

Oysters & Grill

Sjællandsgade 1B; tel: 70 20 61 71; daily from 5.30pm; €

A relaxed, rustic bar-restaurant that does what it says on the tin: go for mussels, oysters, razor clams, soft-shell crabs or shrimp; or grilled steak or sea bream. It has a rough-and-ready concrete-and-vinyl decor but a friendly atmosphere.

Radio

Julius Thomsens Gade 12; tel: 25 10 27 33; http://restaurantradio.dk; Fri–Sat noon–3pm, Tue–Sat from 5.30pm; €€

Radio has won endless plaudits for its fabulous modern-Danish food, and it certainly lives up to expectation. Prices are kept reasonable by packing in the tables, and turning over several sittings every night. On the border of Frederiksberg and Nørrebro, near Forum metro station.

One of many stylish bars in the city

NIGHTLIFE

Here are our picks for some of the hottest bars and clubs in the city. There are always new places popping up – chat to friendly locals to find out about the latest 'in' spots. Many of Copenhagen's best nightspots blur the line between bar and restaurant: often when the nibbles have gone and the kitchen closes, a place will slide smoothly into 'club' mode, staying open late into the night.

Bars and Pubs

Bibendum
Nansensgade 45; tel: 33 33 07 74; www.bibendum.dk; Mon–Sat 4pm–midnight
Wine-lovers should head for this pleasing bar, run by a wine importer. There are 134 varieties to choose from, from all over the globe; and 33 of them are available by the glass. The waiters/bartenders are very knowledgeable, and the small food menu goes well with wining: tapas is a speciality.

The Brass Monkey
Enghavevej 31; tel: 33 22 34 33; www.brassmonkey.dk; Thu 8pm–1am, Fri–Sat until 3am
The 'tiki' bar Brass Monkey comes as close as Scandinavia ever does to dubious taste. Its bartenders wear eye-watering Hawaiian shirts, and its cocktails (based on rum, rum and more rum) are served in goblets shaped like ceramic skulls, zombies and Easter-Island style heads.

Eiffel Bar
Wildersgade 58; tel: 32 57 70 92; daily 9am–3am
This old bar, which has been running in its present form for 50 years, makes no concessions to the 21st century. It's decorated with anachronistic symbols of Paris, and sells cheap beer to retired sailors and local students.

Hviids Vinstue
Kongens Nytorv 19; tel: 33 15 10 64; Mon–Thu 10am–1am, Fri–Sat 10am–2am, Sun 10am–8pm
Cosy, atmospheric and pub-like, Copenhagen's oldest wine bar dates from 1723. In winter, sit in the wood-panelled interior; in summer, sit outside. There is a smoking room if you don't want to brave the elements.

K Bar
Ved Stranden 20; tel: 33 91 92 22; www.k-bar.dk; Mon–Sat 4pm–2am
Close to Højbro Plads, this teeny, tiny Bar promotes 'København, kærlighed & kocktails' (Copenhagen, love and cocktails). It's renowned for martinis – there are 13 different varieties on the menu.

Taphouse
Lavendelstræde 15; tel: 88 87 65 43;

Fans enjoy some live music   *Danes know how to party*

http://taphouse.dk; Mon 3pm–midnight,
Tue–Thu 3pm–2am, Fri–Sat noon–3am,
Sun noon–midnight; happy hour until 6pm
Sun–Thu

The Taphouse, near Rådpladsen, has
the largest selection of on-tap beers
in Europe. It's not just about quantity
either – selected ales come from micro-
and craft breweries the length and
breadth of Denmark and beyond.

Microbreweries
BrewPub
Vestergade 29; tel: 33 32 00 60;
www.brewpub.dk; Mon–Thu noon–
midnight, Fri–Sat noon–2am

This pub, in snug 17th-century premises near to the Rådhus, brews its
own pilsner-style beers in the basement. There are usually seven on tap,
plus another seven from other Danish microbreweries, as well as a huge
choice of bottled beers. True beer afi-
cionados can take a tour of the brewery itself (6pm Mondays; charge;
bookings essential).

Nørrebro Bryghus
Ryesgade 3; tel: 35 30 05 30; Mon–Thu
noon–midnight, Fri–Sat noon–2am

This super microbrewery has won
awards for its beers, which you can
sample at the bar or (in fine weather)
at tables on the street; but it's not all
about getting tipsy in the sunshine.
The Bryghus also offers a creative food
menu specially designed to go with the
hoppy, malty flavour of its amber brews.

Nightclubs
Jolene
Flæsketorvet 81–5; tel: 35 85 69 60; Sun–
Thu 5pm–2am, Fri–Sat until 3am

This lo-fi beery place in the Kødbyen district is run by two Icelandic
women, who bring Iceland's charac-
teristic eccentricity to one of Copenhagen's coolest clubs. It's loud and
odd, with fleamarket decor, party-hard
youngsters. Music on weekdays is
described as 'alternative darksided 7
inches and tunes to watch girls cry',
while at weekends DJs play hiphop,
indie, pop and electronica.

Vega Nightclub
Enghavevej 40; tel: 33 25 70 11;
www.vega.dk; Fri–Sat 11pm–5am; free
before 1am; concerts: charge

This huge complex of bars, clubs and
music venues has everything that you
require for a night out. The mainstream
nightclub has wild lightshows and DJs.
An impressive list of top international
acts, including Prince, Kylie and Bowie,
have performed here.

Jazz Clubs
Mojo's
Løngangstræde 21C; tel: 33 11 64 53;
www.mojo.dk; 8pm–5am; charge

This intimate place is an exciting jazz
venue, known for its laid-back blues
and quality performers. It has live music
every night of the week, but fills up fast:
the best way to get in is to book a table
ahead of time.

Shoppers on Kobmagergade

A–Z

A

Age restrictions

In Denmark, you must be 18 to purchase alcohol and drink in a bar, and 16 to buy alcohol from a shop. The minimum age for driving is 18.

B

Budgeting for your trip

Money-saving tips. Many museums (including the National Museum) are free, or have one day a week where admission is free. A Copenhagen Card (see page 132) can be good value. A free three-hour city tour leaves at 11am from the Rådhus steps – look out for the bright-green umbrella. To save money on a bus tour, hop on bus 11, which runs a circular route around the city centre for the price of a normal bus ticket. Many restaurants offer a good-value *dagens ret* (daily special).

Accommodation. Youth-hostel dormitory bed: 140–250dkk. For a double room without breakfast in high season, expect to pay 1,400dkk for a mid-range hotel and 2,500dkk for a high-end hotel.

Eating out. Three-course evening meal (set menu) in a mid-range restaurant: around 350dkk. Drinks: coffee 35dkk, beer 35–50 dkk and soft drinks 25dkk.

Entertainment. Cinema 90–100dkk; Royal Danish Opera tickets 125–895dkk; nightclub entry 70–350dkk; Tivoli Gardens: 8 years and older 99dkk, multi-ride pass 199dkk.

Flights. Air tickets to Copenhagen vary greatly depending on carrier, flight availability and season. Budget carrier easyJet (www.easyjet.com) has peak-season return flights from London Luton, London Stansted and London Gatwick for around £100. Norwegian Air (www.norwegian.com) has similar flights for around £140.

Business hours

Shops are generally open Mon–Thu 9.30/10am–5.30pm, Fri 9.30/10am–6/7pm; Sat 10am–4pm; Sun noon–4pm. Department stores and large supermarkets often have longer opening hours, as do the kiosks selling newspapers and tobacco.

Museums often open late one night a week (usually Wednesday) and are closed on Monday.

Banks are usually open Mon–Fri 9.30am–4pm; some until 6pm Thu. They are closed on public holidays. If you are looking to exchange money out of usual hours, **Den Danske** Bank at Copenhagen airport is open 6am–10pm and **Forex** at Hovedbånegard is open 8am–9pm.

Waterside Copenhagen in winter

Office hours are usually Mon–Fri 9am–4/4.30pm.

C

Children

Copenhagen is peaceful and safe, with plenty of sights and activities to keep kids amused. Most museums have excellent children's sections, and generally don't charge for under-18s; other attractions offer reduced rates. Highchairs and child-sized portions are widely available in cafés and restaurants. The local transport network in Copenhagen allows two children aged under 12 to travel free with each paying adult.

As well as central sights such as Tivoli (see page 77), there are several major family attractions lying just outside Copenhagen which are well worth visiting.

Bakken and Bellevue Beach

The world's oldest funfair, Bakken (www.bakken.dk; Apr–Aug), attracts 2.5 million visitors a year during its short opening season with rides, sideshows and circus acts. A day pass costs adult/child 249/149dkk. The funfair is set in Dyrehaven, a lovely forested deer park just a short train-ride north of Copenhagen. Alight at Klampenborg, from where the park is a 10-minute walk. Another big family attraction at Klampenborg is the white-sand Bellevue Beach, two min-

utes' walk from the station.

Experimentarium

The interactive science centre Experimentarium (Tuborg Havnevej 7, DK-2900 Hellerup; www.experimentarium.dk), based north of the city in Hellerup, was undergoing a big extension at the time of writing, with building work due for completion in 2015. In the meantime, Experimentarium City (see page 89) has been filling the gap.

National Aquarium Denmark (Den Blå Planet)

Northern Europe's largest aquarium (Danmarks Akvarium; Jacob Fortlingsvej 1; www.denblaaplanet.dk; Mon 10am–9pm, Tue–Sun 10am–6pm; charge) is located out near the airport at Amager. To get here from the city centre, take the 5A bus towards Lufthavnen, alighting at the stop Den Blå Planet, from where the aquarium is a 200-metre/yd walk; or take the metro line M2 to Kastrup, then walk 600 metres/yds down Alleen in an easterly direction.

Climate

Copenhagen is on the same latitude as Moscow and Edinburgh, but the Gulf Stream has a modifying effect on the climate, making it mild for such a northerly city. The winter months, December–February, are cold and windy and there are only five hours of

The Islands Brygge outdoor pool

daylight. February is the coldest month with an average daytime temperature of 1.9°C (35°F), August the warmest at 20.4°C (69°F). In summer there are between 16 and 18 hours of daylight on a clear day.

You can check the latest weather forecasts for Copenhagen and the rest of the country on the Danish Meteorological Institute's website www.dmi.dk.

Clothing

Danes themselves have a relaxed dresscode, with a smart-casual look suitable for nearly every occasion, including the theatre and most dining out. Visitors should bring warm clothes if visiting in winter, as the weather can be chilly. In summer, it's a good idea to bring layers, including a cardigan and a waterproof top layer as the weather can be unpredictable.

Copenhagen is a great city to explore on foot, so comfortable walking shoes are essential. A swimsuit is a must – there are several outdoor pools and artificial beaches in the city, and beautiful white-sand beaches a short train journey away on the eastern and northern coasts of Sjælland.

Crime and safety

Copenhagen is one of the least dangerous cities you could visit. However, it's never a bad thing to secure your personal possessions and not to take any personal risks. Be particularly aware of pickpocketing in crowded areas, such as around Central Station, Rådhuspladsen and the beginning of Strøget (the pedestrian street).

If you are victim of crime, the police are very efficient.

Main police station: Politigården, tel: 33 14 14 48 or tel: 114.

Customs regulations

Visitors arriving from EU countries can bring in 800 cigarettes (or 400 cigarillos or 200 cigars or 1kg of tobacco) and 10 litres of spirits (or 20 litres of fortified wine or 90 litres of table wine or 110 litres of beer). Visitors arriving from outside the EU can bring in 200 cigarettes (or 100 cigarillos, 50 cigars or 250g of tobacco) and 1 litre of spirits (or 2 litres of fortified wine or 4 litres of table wine or 16 litres of beer).

Food articles that are not vacuum-packed by the manufacturer cannot be brought into Denmark. If you are taking money (of any currency) worth over 10,000 euros in or out of the country, you must fill out a customs form.

Non-EU visitors travelling to a non-EU country are eligible for tax refunds: if you have spent over 300dkk in a single shop, ask the cashier for a tax-free form and get it stamped by customs on leaving the country. **Tax Free** Worldwide (www. taxfreeworldwide.com) or **Global Blue** (www.globalblue.com), who have desks in the airport, will refund

A wintery view from the Round Tower

around 20 percent of the purchase price.

D

Disabled travellers

The Danes are generally very thoughtful about customers' needs but not all hotels are suitable for disabled travellers. Contact the Copenhagen tourist office (www.visitcopenhagen.com) for information on hotels, transport, museums and attractions. See also www.visitdenmark.com (look for 'disabled travel' in the 'Denmark A–Z' section).

For wheelchair users travelling by regional train (including the airport) contact the **DSB Handicap Service** (tel: 70 13 14 15, then press '6'; www.dsb.dk). All train and metro stations have lifts and ramps, and most buses have collapsible ramps for the middle doors and a call button. Many cinemas and theatres have hearing loops; call venues for details. Most taxi firms offer specialised transport, but book ahead; try **Taxa4x35** (tel: 35 39 35 35; www.taxa.dk).

E

Electricity

220 volts AC (50 Hz) is the Danish standard. If you are travelling with electrical or electronic devices be sure to bring a two-pin continental adapter with you.

Embassies and consulates

Australia: Dampfærgevej 26, 2nd Floor; tel: 70 26 36 76; www.denmark.embassy.gov.au.
Canada: Kristen Bernikowsgade 1; tel: 33 48 32 00; www.canadainternational.gc.ca.
Republic of Ireland: Østbanegade 21; tel: 35 47 32 00; www.embassyofireland.dk.
UK: Kastelsvej 36/38/40; tel: 35 44 52 00; http://ukindenmark.fco.gov.uk.
USA: Dag Hammarskjölds Allé 24; tel: 33 41 71 00; http://denmark.usembassy.gov.

Emergencies

Emergency services (police, fire, ambulance): 112.
Politivagten (local police): 114 or 33 14 14 48.
Airport police: 32 31 34 00.
Out-of-hours medical care: After hours (4pm–8am) and during weekends, contact the on-call GP on 38 69 38 69. There is also a 24-hour, 365-day helpline (tel: 1813) staffed by nurses who can advise on medical questions, and tell you which emergency clinic has the shortest waiting time.
Dental emergency: Tandlægevagten, Oslo Plads 14, is a walk-in centre for out-of-hours dental emergencies, open Mon–Fri 8–9.30pm, Sat–Sun and public holidays 10am–noon and 8–9.30pm. Cash payment only.

F

Festivals and events

For an up-to-the-minute guide to what's on, visit the tourist office (see page 132) or pick up a copy of *Copenhagen This Week*. For public holidays, see page 131.

February
Vinterjazz. Two weeks of winter jazz. http://jazz.dk.
Frost Festival. A month of pop/electronic gigs in unusual venues. http://frostfestival.dk.
Shrovetide. Parades and carnival festivities, centred around Rådhuspladsen and the Nationalmuseet. Also at Dragør on Amager island.

April
Queen's birthday. Crowds gather on 16 April outside Amalienborg Slot at noon for a balcony appearance.
CPH PIX. Two-week international film festival. www.cphpix.dk.

May
May Day. Marches and brass bands converge on Fælled Park.
Copenhagen Marathon. Held in mid-May. www.copenhagenmarathon.dk.
Distortion 300,000 ravers join a city-wide party (late May/early June). www.cphdistortion.dk.
Copenhagen Carnival. Colourful Latin-style processions and hundreds of bands during the Whitsun Holiday.

June
St Hans Eve. Bonfires in parks and on beaches mark the longest day (23 June).
Roskilde Festival. Northern Europe's biggest rock festival takes place in late June. www.roskilde-festival.dk.

July
Copenhagen Jazz Festival. Bebop and beyond, on stages, in pubs and on the streets. http://jazz.dk.

August
Copenhagen Historic Grand Prix. Vintage cars rally. www.chgp.dk.
Copenhagen Pride. Five-day GLBT event culminating in a colourful parade. http://copenhagenpride.dk.
Kulturhavn. Harbour-based festival, with music, dancing and family fun. http://kulturhavn.dk.

September
Golden Days Festival. Celebrates different eras of Copenhagen's history with cultural events. http://goldendaysfestival.dk
Blues Festival. Two weeks of concerts across the city. www.copenhagenbluesfestival.dk.

October
Culture Night. Museums, galleries, churches and theatres open their doors to the public after dark. www.kulturnatten.dk.

Christmas at Tivoli

November–December
Tivoli Christmas Market. Tivoli transforms into a winter wonderland.

G

Gay travellers

Denmark was the first country to recognise same-sex marriages and is a welcoming place. For advice and information, contact **LGBT Danmark** (tel: 33 13 19 48; www.lgbt.dk). *Out & About* magazine (www.outandabout. dk) features listings for bars, nightlife and events, including Copenhagen Pride (www.copenhagenpride. dk) in mid-August. Copenhagen Gay Life (www.copenhagen-gay-life.dk) is another good resource.

H

Health

The Danish medical system will assist anyone in an emergency; however you should take out travel insurance before you leave. British nationals should take a European Health Insurance Card (EHIC; www.ehic.org.uk). Emergency hospital treatment is free, as long as you have not travelled to Denmark intending to receive treatment and are too ill to return home.

Prescription drugs for personal use (30 days' worth for Schengen residents, 15 days' worth for non-Schengen visitors) may be brought to Denmark: try to bring along your doctor's prescription too. Pharmacies are listed in the phone book under Apoteker and designated by a green 'A' for Apotek. General opening hours are 9am–5.30pm and until 1pm on Sat. Credit cards are not accepted in pharmacies. Full payment is required for all medications.
Late-night opening: Steno Apotek (24 hours); Vesterbrogade 6C (opposite main station); tel: 33 14 82 66.

L

Lost property

For items lost on the bus, go to www. moviatrafik.dk, click 'Kontakt', then 'Hittegods', then type in the bus number to find the correct contact telephone number. Items lost on the local (S) train are kept for one month before being handed over to the police: tel: 48 29 87 00. For lost property at the airport, tel: 32 31 22 84. For all other losses, ring the police station at Slotsherrensvej 113; tel: 38 74 88 22.

M

Maps

The tourist board and most hotels offer free city maps with sights and sometimes bus routes marked on them. The Discover Green Copenhagen map shows eco-friendly restaurants, bars and activities. If you need a street index, the Insight Copenhagen Fleximap is a good option.

Media

Newspapers and magazines: English-language newspapers and magazines are widely available. The kiosk at Central Station sells foreign-language publications, and there is a good selection at Magasin du Nord (Kongens Nytorv13) and Illums (Østergade 52–54) department stores. The English-language weekly *Copenhagen Post* (www.cphpost.dk; free from tourist offices and some hotels) has local news and listings. Denmark's main newspapers are *Berlingske Tidende, Ekstra Bladet, Jyllands-Posten* and *Politiken.*

Television: Cable and satellite television is widely available. Foreign films are rarely dubbed into Danish and appear in the original version with subtitles.

Money

Cash machines

ATMs are open 24 hours and can usually be found outside banks and metro stations. The smallest amount that you can draw out is 100dkk.

Credit cards

Visa, Mastercard and American Express are widely accepted but usually attract a fee. Many smaller, independent retailers (including pharmacies) do not accept them, or request a surcharge (up to 4 percent of the bill), so do not rely wholly on plastic. If your credit card gets lost or stolen, call the Danish PBS/Nets 24-hour hotline, tel: 44 89 27 50, to block your card.

Currency

Denmark uses Danish kroner (dkk). One krone is divided into 100 øre. Danish notes come in 1,000dkk, 500dkk, 200dkk, 100dkk and 50dkk. Coins are in denominations of 20dkk, 10dkk, 5dkk 2dkk, 1dkk, and 50 øre (half a krone).

Tax

Danish VAT is called MOMS and is set at 25 percent. It's always included in the bill. Non-EU visitors can claim a tax refund if they spend over 300dkk in a single shop displaying the Global Tax-Free Shopping sign. Ask the cashier for a tax-free form, then take it to Tax Free Worldwide (www.taxfreeworldwide.com) or Global Blue (www.globalblue.com) desks in the airport and large department stores for a 20 percent refund. Alternatively, you can post your tax-free form.

Post

Post offices usually open Mon–Fri 9/10am–5/6pm, Sat (if open) 9/10am–noon. There are several central post offices, including at Central Station (Hovedbanegård; www.postdanmark.dk), which has the longest opening

hours: Mon–Fri 8am–9pm, Sat–Sun 10am–4pm.

When buying postcards from stands and souvenir shops, you can get the appropriate stamps on the spot. Danish postboxes are bright red and stand out cheerfully. 'A Prioritaire' mail is the fastest international option.

Public and school holidays

Though Denmark's banks, offices and major shops close on public holidays, museums, cafés and tourist attractions will mostly be open. Christmas Eve and New Year's Eve are not official holidays, but most shops, businesses and attractions close on those days too. For festivals, see page 128.

1 January *Nytårsdag* New Year's Day
5 June (half-day) *Grundslovsdag* Constitution Day
25/26 December Christmas
Moveable dates (according to where Easter falls):
Skærtorsdag **Maundy Thursday**
Langfredag **Good Friday**
Anden påskedag **Easter Monday**
Store Bededag **General Prayer Day (fourth Friday after Easter)**
Kristi himmelfartsdag **Ascension Day**
Anden pinsedag **Whit Monday**

R

Religion

Denmark's Constitution provides for freedom of religion. The evangelical Lutheran church is the state church. Officially, 78 percent of Danes are members, but church attendance is low and many Danes are agnostic or atheist. Muslims make up the second largest religious community (four percent of the population).

T

Telephones

Local Danish numbers have eight digits. There are no area codes.
Local directory assistance: 118.
International directory assistance: 113.
International calls from Denmark: 00 + country code + area code + personal number.
International calls to Denmark: 00 + 45 + personal number.
International country codes: Britain +44, France +33, Germany +49, Ireland +353, Italy +39, Japan +81, Norway +47, Sweden +46, USA +1.
Public telephones: Most public telephones take pre-paid cards, available in 30dkk, 50dkk and 100dkk denominations, from kiosks, supermarkets and petrol stations; some take credit cards and coins (but not 50 øre coins). No change is given. Collect calls to the US are not possible.
Mobile telephones: Danish mobile phones operate on the 900/1800 Mhz GSM network, on which most unlocked European phones will work. US visitors will only be able to use their cellphone

Copenhagen is one of Europe's most cycle-friendly cities

in Denmark if it is a tri-band phone that can switch bands.

Time zones

Denmark is one hour ahead of GMT. Summer time, when the clocks go forward one hour, runs from the last Sunday in March to the last Sunday in October.

Tourist information

The **Wonderful Copenhagen** tourist office (Vesterbrogade 4A; tel: 70 22 24 42; www.visitcopenhagen.com; www.visitdenmark.dk; July–Aug Mon–Sat 9am–8pm, Sun 10am–6pm; May–June Mon–Sat 9am–6pm, Sun 10am–2pm; Sept–Apr Mon–Fri 9am–4pm, Sat 9am–2pm) is opposite the Tivoli entrance. You can get brochures, book hotels, tickets and tours, and drink coffee. Staff here speak English and there is free Wi-fi. You can also purchase the Copenhagen Card from here. The tourist office has produced an official App, iSpot Copenhagen (available on iTunes and Google Play), with lots of information plus a current-events calendar.

A **Copenhagen Card** (CPH Card; www.copenhagencard.com) gives entry to 72 attractions in the Copenhagen area, offers some discounts and also entitles you to free travel on trains, buses and the metro (this includes public transport to/from the airport, and also to Roskilde, Helsingør and the art galleries in Route 14). They are valid for 24/48/72/120 hours (339/469/559/779dkk for adults; 179/239/289/379dkk for children aged 10–15). Up to two children under the age of 10 are allowed free with each adult card. You can buy the cards online or at the tourist office, airport and main railway stations.

The English newspaper the **Copenhagen Post** (published on Fridays) has a useful weekly guide to what's on.

Transport

Getting to Copenhagen is easy, with many airlines offering daily flights, as well as direct rail services from Sweden and Germany. Access from the airport is also very straightforward with train, bus and taxi options, which will take you to the city centre. There are also ferry services to Copenhagen.

Getting there
By plane

Budget airlines offering flights to Copenhagen include easyJet (www.easyjet.com) and Norwegian (www.norwegian.com). Copenhagen Airport, Kastrup (www.cph.dk) lies 12km (7.5 miles) southeast of the city centre, on Amager Island. There are trains to Hovedbanegård, Copenhagen's Central Station; and the metro runs roughly every four minutes into the city centre. Both leave from Terminal 3 (where all passengers go for baggage reclaim and customs), take about 14 minutes and cost about 36dkk.

Hovedbanegård (Central Station)

There is a **taxi rank** at Terminal 3. The 20-minute taxi journey to the centre costs around 250–350dkk depending on the time and includes VAT and tip.

By train

There are four direct trains daily to/from Hamburg, Germany; and trains run every 10 minutes to/from Sweden, arriving at Hovedbanegård (Central Station). The S-tog (local) trains also leave from the Central Station and run on a separate network.

For German rail enquiries and bookings, contact **DB Bahn**: tel: +49 1805 996 633 (International); +44 8718 808 066 (UK); www.bahn.de.

For Swedish rail journeys, contact **SJ**: tel: +46 771 757 575; www.sj.se.

For Danish and outgoing international rail enquiries and bookings, contact **Danish Rail** (DSB): tel: 70 13 14 15; www.dsb.dk.

By bus

The biggest operator of scheduled coach services to/from Denmark is Eurolines: tel: +45 33 88 70 00 (Copenhagen), +44 8717 818 181 (UK); www.eurolines-travel.com. Buses stop at Copenhagen's Central Station.

By ferry

The new ferry terminal (www.cphport.dk), close to Nordhavn train station, is linked to the city centre by shuttle bus. **DFDS Seaways** (Denmark tel: +45 33 42 30 10; www.dfdsseaways.com) operate ferries from Oslo (16 hours) to Copenhagen. The Danish company Regina Line (www.reginaline.dk) plans to operateferries from Harwich in the UK to Esbjerg from 2015. Ferries from Germany with **Scandlines** (Denmark tel: + 45 33 15 15 15; Germany tel: +49 (0)381 77 88 77 66; www.scandlines.com) arrive at Rødby, Rønne and Gedser.

By cruise ship

Cruise ships dock at one of four cruise terminals, Langelinie Quay, Nordre Toldbod, Freeport (Frihavnen) and Ocean Quay (Oceankaj), all in the north harbour (Nordhavn). You can walk into the city along the waterside, or bus No. 26 links the terminals with the Central Station, Rådhuspladsen (City Hall Square) and Kongens Nytorv.

By car: Drivers arriving in Rødby from Germany (Puttgarden) should take the E47.

Both the Storebælt bridge/tunnel from Funen to Sjælland, and the Øresund bridge from Malmö to Copenhagen levy a toll.

Getting around

For fare purposes, the city is divided into zones. Fares are charged on the number of zones that you pass through (minimum two).

The bus, harbour bus, metro and S-tog (local train) all use the same tickets so you can change between them without buying a new one. The cheapest options are to buy a discount Klippekort of 10 tickets (which can be shared between several people) or a

A busy cycle lane

24-hour ticket. Alternatively, if you have a Copenhagen Card (see page 132), local travel is free.

Tickets can be bought on the bus, at ticket offices or vending machines. Discount cards, with an average saving of 40 percent cannot be bought on the bus.

Individual tickets have a time limit of an hour for two zones (adult 24dkk/under 16s 12dkk) and you must clip your ticket when you get on the bus or on the train platform before you get on.

Using the night bus or the metro between 1am and 5am costs double the daytime fare.

By bus

Buses are operated by Movia (www.movia trafik.dk). They are regular, although the city is so compact that it's usually easier to walk. Nearly all stop at either Rådhuspladsen (City Hall Square) or Hovedbanegård (Central Station).

Buses run daily between 6am and 12.30am and there are additional night buses from Rådhuspladsen (City Hall Square) to the suburbs.

Buses are yellow and you get on at the front and off at the back.

By S-tog

The S-tog (local train) connects Copenhagen with other towns on Sjælland. Tickets are available at all S-tog stations.

By metro

The award-winning driverless metro (tel: 70 15 16 15; www.m.dk; Mon–Fri 8am–4pm) operates a frequent service: every 4–6 minutes in the daytime, and every 15–20 minutes through the night. Currently there are two lines, M1 runs from Vanløse Station to West Amager, and M2 runs from Vanløse Station to Copenhagen Airport in East Amager. Both lines take you through the heart of the city.

The ambitious Cityringen circle extension, which will create two new lines and 17 new stations, is due to open in 2019.

By bicycle

The Danes are avid cyclists and bicycles enjoy equal status with cars on Copenhagen's roads. When using the cycleways, keep to the right. Helmets are optional, but cycling without lights at night, under the influence of alcohol or jumping red lights can earn you an instant 500dkk fine.

You can join in by borrowing one of Copenhagen's electric, puncture-free, GPS-fitted **Bycyklen** (www.bycyklen. dk), available at various docking stations around the inner city for 25dkk per hour. You will need to set up an account via the website before you travel. Bicycles are widely available from hostels, hotels and private hire shops, with rental varying from free to 80–150dkk per day; 270–530dkk per week.

Bike rental companies include **Kobenhavns Cykelbørs** (Gothersgade 157; tel: 33 14 07 17; Mon–Fri 8.30am– 5.30pm; Sat 10am–2pm; also May–Aug

Copenhagen's bright yellow buses are easy to spot

Sat 6–9pm and Sun 10am–2pm and 6–9pm) and **Baisikeli** (Turesensgade 10; tel: 26 70 02 29; daily 10am–6pm; http://baisikeli.dk), which uses its profits to ship bicycles – over 5000 at the last count – to Mozambique. **Biking Copenhagen** (tel: 30 11 30 86; www.bikingcopenhagen.com) operate bike tours of the city.

Harbour buses

The blue-and-yellow harbour buses follow two routes. The 991/992 sails from Nordre Toldbod (near the Little Mermaid) to Teglholmen, in the southwest, stopping at the Black Diamond, Knippel's Bridge (Christianshavn), Nyhavn and the Opera House. The 993 zips between Nyhavn, Experimentarium City and the Opera House. Harbour buses run daily from 6am–6/7pm, and accept local transport tickets. They are free with the Copenhagen Card.

By car

Cars are not practical in Copenhagen, but if you do hire a car, you must be over 20 years old and hold a valid licence. Some car firms may stipulate that you have to be over 25.

Danes drive on the right and speed limits are 110 or 130 kmh (66 or 80 mph) on motorways, 80 kmh (50 mph) on other roads and 50 kmh (30 mph) in a built-up area. Take a UK or EU driving licence and a warning triangle, and wear a seat belt at all times.

Headlights must be dipped at all times. Be aware of cycle lanes on both sides of the road in towns. *Parkering Forbudt* means No Parking.

Car hire companies

Budget: tel: 33 55 05 00, www.budget.dk

Sixt: tel: 32 48 11 00, www.dk.sixt.com

Taxis

Taxis can be identified by the sign on the roof with the word FRI, meaning 'free'. Most drivers speak English and often some German. They can give you receipts and you can pay with a credit card. The basic fare for a taxi is 37dkk, then 15.25dkk for each kilometre thereafter at off-peak times, 19.15dkk per kilometre Fri–Sat 11pm–7am. Tips are not expected, but it is usual to round up the final amount.

Dantaxi: tel: 70 25 25 25.

Taxa 4x35: tel: 35 35 35 35. Also provides taxis equipped with wheelchair lifts and ramps for disabled passengers (tel: 35 39 35 35; www.taxa.dk).

Visas

Citizens of the EU do not need a visa; other visitors should check with their country. Visitors not obliged to have a visa are allowed to stay in Denmark for up to 90 days. See www.nyidanmark.dk.

Weights and measures

The metric system is used in Denmark.

LANGUAGE

English is widely spoken and understood. Danish is perhaps the most difficult northern-European language for relating the written word to speech; it's almost impossible to pronounce simply by reading the words, as many syllables are swallowed rather than spoken. Thus the island of Amager becomes Am-air, with the 'g' disappearing, but in a distinctively Danish way difficult for the visitor to imitate. The letter 'd' becomes something like a 'th', but with the tongue placed behind the lower teeth, not the upper. And the letter 'r' is, again, swallowed.

Despite their differences of grammar, usage and vocabulary, Danes, Norwegians and Swedes are able to understand one another. In a tripartite conversation, each will speak his or her own national language.

Vowels
a – aa, as in bar
å – aw, as in paw
æ – as in pear
e – as in bed
i – ee, as in sleep
ø – as in fur

Useful words and phrases

General
yes/no *ja/nej*
big/little *stor/lille*
good/bad *god/dårlig*
possible/impossible *muligt/umuligt*
hot/cold *varm/kold*
much/little *meget/lidt*
many/few *mange/få*
and/or *og/eller*
please/thank you *vær så venlig/tak*
I *jeg*
you (formal) *du (de)*
he/she *han/hun*
it *den/det*
we *vi*
you (formal) *I (de)*
they *de*
foreigner *udlænding*

Numbers
1 *en/et*
2 *to*
3 *tre*
4 *fire*
5 *fem*
6 *seks*
7 *syv*
8 *otte*
9 *ni*
10 *ti*
20 *tyve*
30 *tredive*
40 *fyrre*
50 *halvtreds*
60 *tres*
70 *halvfjerds*
80 *firs*
90 *halvfems*
100 *hundrede*

Books in a Copenhagen café

Food and drink
breakfast *morgenmad*
lunch (break) *frokost (pause)*
dinner *middag*
tea *te*
coffee *kaffe*
beer *fadøl*

Getting around
left *venstre*
right *højre*
street *(en) gade/vej*
bicycle (path) *(en) cykel (sti)*
car *(en) bil*
bus/coach *(en) bus*
train *(et) tog*
ferry *(en) færge*
bridge *(en) bro*
traffic light *(et) trafiklys*
square *(et) torv*
north *nord*
south *syd*
east *øst*
west *vest*

Money
How much is it? *Hvad koster det?*
Can I pay with… *Må jeg betale med…*
travellers' cheques *rejsechecks*
money *penge*
notes/coins *sedler/mønter*
Please may I have *Må jeg få*
the bill? *regningen?*
May I have a *Må jeg få en*
receipt? *kvittering?*
bank *(en) bank*
exchange *veksle*
exchange rate *kurs*

business hours *åbningstider*
open *åben*
closed *lukket*

Medical
pharmacy *(et) apotek*
hospital *(et) hospital*
casualty *(en) skadestue*
doctor *(en) læge*

Time
What time is it? *Hvad er klokken?*
good morning *godmorgen*
good day/evening *goddag*
goodnight *godaften/godnat*
today *i dag*
tomorrow *i morgen*

Calendar
Monday *mandag*
Tuesday *tirsdag*
Wednesday *onsdag*
Thursday *torsdag*
Friday *fredag*
Saturday *lørdag*
Sunday *søndag*
January *januar*
February *februar*
March *marts*
April *april*
May *maj*
June *juni*
July *juli*
August *august*
September *september*
October *oktober*
November *november*
December *december*

BOOKS AND FILM

The Danes have always been a nation of storytellers: as far back as the third century, runes jostled their way around the edges of stones, proclaiming the deeds of warriors and kings. In the 13th century, Saxo Grammaticus created Denmark's first major literary work *Gesta Danorum* (*History of the Danes*), from where Shakespeare stole his idea for *Hamlet*. During the Danish Golden Age (1800–50), Hans Christian Andersen strode the world stage and Søren Kierkegaard wrestled with the meaning of life. The two best-known authors of the 20th century are aristocrat Karen Blixen, and more recently former ballet-dancer Peter Høeg.

Denmark is perhaps better known for its film and TV productions. Homegrown Danish cinema really took off during World War II, when the occupying Germans banned the import of foreign films. In the 1990s, in protest against overblown Hollywood productions, Lars von Trier and Thomas Vinterberg launched the Dogme 95 manifesto, whose rigid and complex rules were paradoxically used to create simple, naturalistic films.

Books

History

A History of the Vikings by Gwyn Jones. A compelling history of Viking society.

The Vikings by Else Roesdahl. Another good exploration of the Norse traders, raiders and explorers.

The Battle of Copenhagen 1801 by Ole Feldbæk. How Napoleonic politics led to the brutal bombardment of Copenhagen by the British.

The English Dane: From King of Iceland to Tasmanian Convict by Sarah Bakewell. A fascinating account of archblagger Jorgen Jorgenson, the self-appointed King of Iceland.

***Danish Dynamite: The Story of Football's Greatest Cult Team* by** Rob Smyth, Lars Eriksen and Mike Gibbons. Tracing the rise of the coolest football team on earth.

Non-fiction

Out of Africa by Karen Blixen (aka Isak Dinesen). Vivid autobiography of a Danish aristocrat, later made into a Hollywood film starring Meryl Streep.

Early Spring by Tove Ditlevsen. A funny, poignant account of growing up in working-class Vesterbro in the 1920s.

Either/Or, Fear and Trembling and ***The Concept of Anxiety*** by Søren Kierkegaard. Ponder the imponderables with Denmark's favourite existentialist philosopher.

Quantum: Einstein, Bohr and the Great Debate About the Nature of Reality by Manjit Kumar. A rollicking read, focusing on a decades-long argument between Einstein and Nobel-Prize-winning physicist Niels Bohr.

Sofie Gråbøl as Detective Sarah Lund in The Killing

Danish Modern by Andrew Hollingsworth. A history of Danish design, from the 18th century to the present.

Fiction
The Complete Fairy Tales by Hans Christian Andersen. Classic childhood tales, such as 'The Little Mermaid' and 'The Ugly Duckling'.
Seven Gothic Tales by Karen Blixen (aka Isak Dinesen). Dreamy, romantic and melancholy stories of fate and death.
The Exception by Christian Jungersen. A best-selling psychological thriller, told from four different viewpoints.
The Visit of The Royal Physician by Per Olov Enquist. Madness, passion and intrigue in the 18th-century Danish court.
Miss Smilla's Feeling for Snow by Peter Høeg. A cool, haunting thriller. The death of a child sets the half-Danish, half-Greenlandic Miss Smilla on a relentless hunt for the truth.
The History of Danish Dreams by Peter Høeg. A magical-realist account of Denmark's transition to a modern welfare state.
Silence in October by Jens Christian Grøndahl. The end of a marriage brings dark reflections in this stream-of-consciousness novel.
We, the Drowned by Carsten Jensen. This brilliant novel follows three generations of sailors from the Danish town of Marstal.

Film and TV

Babette's Feast (Babettes Gæstebud), 1987, dir. Gabriel Axel. Sumptuous Oscar-winning film based on a short story by Karen Blixen, set in Jutland.
Pelle the Conqueror (Pelle Erobreren), 1987, dir. Bille August. Award-winning film about a Swedish father and son immigrating to Bornholm.
Breaking the Waves, 1996, dir. Lars von Trier. A psychologically damaged Scottish woman is urged by her husband to have sex with other men after an accident leaves him paralysed.
Festen, 1996, dir. Thomas Vinterberg. Family secrets emerge at a birthday celebration. The first of the Dogme 95 films.
The Idiots (Idioterne), 1998, dir. Lars von Trier. A group of Copenhageners test the boundaries of "normality" in a Dogme 95 film that still has the power to shock.
After the Wedding (Efter Brylluppet), 2007, dir. Susanne Bier. Oscar-nominated film about a Danish director of an Indian orphanage.
In a Better World (Hævnen), 2011, dir. Susanne Bier. Oscar-winning thriller that moves between small-town Denmark and a Sudanese refugee camp.
A Royal Affair (En kongelig affære), 2012, dir. Nikolaj Arcel. Superb historical drama about the affair between Johann Struensee and Queen Caroline Matilda.
A Hjacking (Kapringen), 2012, dir. Tobias Lindholm. A Danish freighter is captured by Somali pirates in this ultra-tense hostage drama.
The Hunt (Jagten), 2013, dir. Thomas Vinterberg. Tensions escalate in a close-knit Danish community when a kindergarten teacher is suspected of abuse.

ABOUT THIS BOOK

This *Explore Guide* has been produced by the editors of Insight Guides, whose books have set the standard for visual travel guides since 1970. With top-quality photography and authoritative recommendations, these guidebooks bring you the very best routes and itineraries in the world's most exciting destinations.

BEST ROUTES

The routes in the book provide something to suit all budgets, tastes and trip lengths. As well as covering the destination's many classic attractions, the itineraries track lesser-known sights, and there are also excursions for those who want to extend their visit outside the city. The routes embrace a range of interests, so whether you are an art fan, a gourmet, a history buff or have kids to entertain, you will find an option to suit.

We recommend reading the whole of a route before setting out. This should help you to familiarise yourself with it and enable you to plan where to stop for refreshments – options are shown in the 'Food and Drink' box at the end of each tour.

For our pick of the tours by theme, consult Recommended Routes for… (see pages 4–5).

INTRODUCTION

The routes are set in context by this introductory section, giving an overview of the destination to set the scene, plus background information on food and drink, shopping and more, while a succinct history timeline highlights the key events over the centuries.

DIRECTORY

Also supporting the routes is a Directory chapter, with a clearly organised A–Z of practical information, our pick of where to stay while you are there and select restaurant listings; these eateries complement the more low-key cafés and restaurants that feature within the routes and are intended to offer a wider choice for evening dining. Also included here are some nightlife listings, plus a handy language guide and our recommendations for books and films about the destination.

ABOUT THE AUTHORS

Antonia Cunningham has written several books, including two books on world art and the Impressionists, and five on Copenhagen and Denmark. She lives in London with her partner Nick and son Benjamin, to both of whom she dedicates this book. This edition was updated by Fran Parnell, whose passion for Scandinavia began while studying Norse and Celtic at Cambridge University. She has written guides to Iceland, Sweden, Denmark and Scandinavia.

CONTACT THE EDITORS

We hope you find this Explore Guide useful, interesting and a pleasure to read. If you have any questions or feedback on the text, pictures or maps, please do let us know. If you have noticed any errors or outdated facts, or have suggestions for places to include on the routes, we would be delighted to hear from you. Please drop us an email at hello@insightguides.com. Thanks!

CREDITS

Explore Copenhagen
Contributors: Antonia Cunningham,
Fran Parnell
Commissioning Editor: Rachel Lawrence
Pictures: Tom Smyth
Map Production: updated by Apa
Cartography Department
Production: Rebeka Davies and Aga Bylica
Photo credits: Alamy 28/29, 139; Apa
Publications 61; Carlsberg 31L; David Hall/
Apa Publications 34/35, 120, 134, 135,
136/137; Design Hotels 41L; Getty Images
1, 2/3T, 23, 26/27T; Hotel 27 40/41,
102MC, 102/103T; Ib Rasmussen 40; iStock
5M, 12/13, 24, 25, 44/45, 50, 51L, 53L,
55, 66, 69, 72, 76, 90, 125; Leonardo 28,
102MR, 102ML; Rudy Hemmingsen/Apa
Publications 5MR, 20, 30/31, 32, 34, 35L,
36, 38, 38/39, 39L, 42, 44, 45L, 48, 49L,
50/51, 52, 52/53, 54, 56, 56/57, 57L, 58,
58/59, 59L, 70, 70/71, 71L, 73, 74, 75,
76/77, 77L, 78, 79, 80L, 80/81, 81, 82,
82/83, 83L, 84, 85L, 84/85, 86, 86/87,
87L, 88, 89, 91, 92/93, 92L, 93, 94, 95, 96,
97, 98, 99, 100, 100/101; SMK Foto 60, 62,
63, 64, 65; VEGA 21; Wonderful Copenhagen 2ML, 2MC, 2MR, 2MR, 2MC, 2ML, 4TL,
4MC, 4ML, 4BC, 5T, 5MR, 6ML, 6MC, 6ML,
6MC, 6MR, 6MR, 6/7T, 8, 9, 10, 10/11, 11L,
14, 14/15, 15L, 16, 17, 18, 19, 22, 26ML,
26MC, 26MR, 26ML, 26MC, 26MR, 29L, 30,
33, 36/37, 37L, 43, 46, 47, 48/49, 67, 68T,
68B, 101L, 102ML, 102MR, 102MC, 104,
104/105, 105L, 106, 106/107, 107L, 108,
108/109, 109L, 110, 110/111, 111L, 112,
113, 114, 114/115, 115L, 116, 117, 118,
119, 121, 122, 122/123, 123L, 124, 126,
127, 128/129, 130/131, 132, 133

Cover credits: Corbis (main); David Hall/Apa
Publications (bottom)

Printed by CTPS – China
© 2015 Apa Publications (UK) Ltd

DISTRIBUTION

Worldwide
APA Publications GmbH & Co. Verlag KG
(Singapore branch)
7030 Ang Mo Kio Ave 5, 08-65
Northstar @ AMK, Singapore 569880
Email: apasin@singnet.com.sg
UK and Ireland
Dorling Kindersley Ltd (a Penguin Company)
80 Strand, London, WC2R 0RL, UK
Email: sales@uk.dk.com
US
Ingram Publisher Services
One Ingram Blvd, PO Box 3006, La Vergne,
TN 37086-1986
Email: ips@ingramcontent.com
Australia and New Zealand
Woodslane
10 Apollo St, Warriewood NSW 2102,
Australia
Email: info@woodslane.com.au

INDEX

MAP LEGEND

★ Place of interest

● Start of tour

🛈 Tourist information

I Statue/monument

→ Tour & route direction

❶ Recommended sight

✉ Main post office

🚌 Main bus station

❷ Recommended
restaurant/café

⚶ Viewpoint

Park

Important building

Hotel

Transport hub

Market/store

Pedestrian area

Urban area